'Milk my Ewes and Weep'

JOYCE FUSSEY

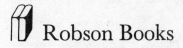 Robson Books

To the neighbours, bless 'em

First published in Great Britain in hardback in 1978 by Paul
Elek Ltd. This paperback edition published by Robson Books Ltd,
Bolsover House, 5 – 6 Clipstone Street, London W1P 7EB in 1988.
Reprinted 1990
Copyright © 1978 by Joyce Fussey

British Library Cataloguing in Publication Data

Fussey, Joyce
   Milk my ewes and weep.
   1. Agriculture—England—North York
Moors
   I. Title
   630'.92'4   S457.N6/

ISBN 0-86051-497-8

Printed in Great Britain by Billing & Sons Ltd., Worcester.

Contents

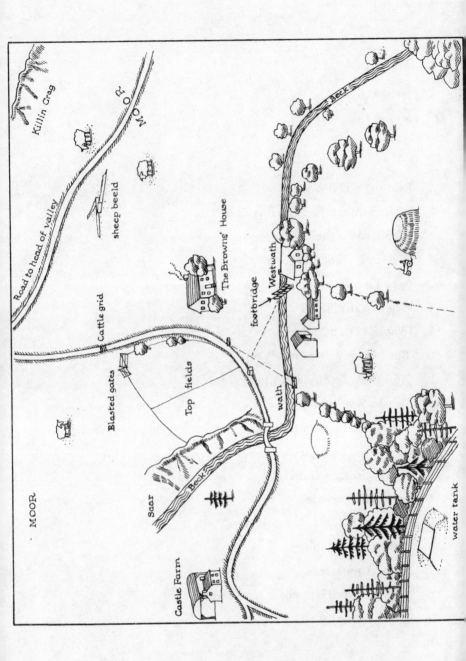

1 Burning our Boats

'It was never like this in Bellfield Avenue,' I sobbed wildly, clawing at swags of rusty barbed wire and struggling to keep over-end whilst wading thigh deep in sheep. '*Will* you stand up, you blasted thing. *Will* you . . . oh, to hell with the blasted gate!'

At the top of a one-in-four field and opening onto the moor, the gate, a euphemism for crooked hurdle, streamed out horizontally from my ravaged hands. Below, along the winding river valley the wind hurtled through the alders with the speed and sound of a Phantom Jet. The walls of the Scar, a glacial ravine, echoed with the fury, swallowing the usual muted roar of water. On the field side of the boundary wall two or three rowans threshed dementedly and over on the moor bracken bowed in undulating submission.

'Other people have proper gates and posts to hang them on,' I screamed into the wind. 'Why can't we?' I've got into this habit of talking to myself because sheep are poor conversationalists.

On happier occasions the gate was supported by binder-twine tied to anything convenient, and in its turn held up four more hurdles of equal dependence, all linked together by sagging tangles of band like children holding hands in Ring-o-roses. They formed a pentagonal sheep pen. One of the hurdles opened out onto the moor and sometimes, accidentally, they all did and the sheep got out — or in: whichever they shouldn't.

'All fall down!' shrieked the wind. Down went the hurdles like a pack of cards and a tide of happy sheep swept out onto the moor carrying me on its crest. Craftily, the last ewe hooked her horn inside my boot and added my prostrate form to those of the gates.

It hadn't always been like this. Six months before my conflict with the blasted gate, as it is now officially known, we had lived a normal, rational life in Kingston-upon-Hull, where Gordon worked in a garage and I kept having baby sons as an excuse to read *Winnie the Pooh* again, and was quite incapable of telling gates to go to hell, however blasted. Every summer we spent a fortnight in a bungalow on the North York Moors, and that was the beginning of it all.

The bungalow was at Westwath, a little farm situated in a bowl-shaped depression whose sides were hung with woods and small fields and rimmed with heather and bracken. A sparkling beck girded the farmhouse and buildings, and was crossed by a high narrow footbridge and a wider concrete ford — known, like others in this part of the country, by the Old Norse name *wath*. Billowy treetops hid the farm from the road and it was unsuspected by most passing travellers. To us it was an enchanted place to dream about during long town-bound months. We would snatch any excuse to run up there at weekends: to pay the deposit for next summer's holiday, to buy heather-scented honey and, on the last significant occasion, to replace a cup broken on the last morning of the past holiday.

On this memorable afternoon we had returned the cup and were holding others filled with tea. As we marvelled at the enormous fire — logs a couple of yards long rested on the black turf-plate, one end burning fiercely, the other projecting halfway across the room to be kicked periodically towards the blaze, sending out a shower of sparks which seriously threatened the black, clipped rug — more visitors arrived.

To our acute dismay we learned that on the following Wednesday the farm was to be sold by auction and that the newcomers were two of the many prospective buyers who trailed their muddy boots through the living room and clattered up the stairs. The young man, stocky and fiery-faced with a combination of the weather, embarrassment and the tightness of his Sunday suit, escorted a plump fiancée whose mirth threatened to overcome her when Mrs Rust suggested that they should inspect the bedrooms. They were still up there when the next aspirant arrived, a loquacious lady flushed with the excitement of the chase. It was *exactly* what they were looking for, she cried. The birds, the trees, the peace. Oh, what it must be like in spring! Vociferously she went off to do the grand tour and we managed to scan the estate agent's notice which she had dropped on the table.

'Three bedrooms,' it said. 'Two living rooms with hand-carved stone fireplace surrounds. Kitchen. Bathroom. Piped for calor gas. Two WCs.' Someone had underlined the last item and scribbled underneath, 'What holidays we could have!' We didn't laugh, we could hardly speak. We had only one thought in our heads. We wanted Westwath and hadn't the faintest idea what we could do about it.

We dropped the notice on the table as the woman re-entered the room. She was still enthusiastic and depressingly optimistic. Her husband was in America, she said. She would wire him the minute she got home and she *knew* he'd tell her to go ahead. Her gleaming smile swept the room. I bet she was dying to see her folksy pine dresser in that setting. The second-best one, of course. After all it was only to be a holiday house.

The settling soundwaves were almost tangible as she departed at last and with a pleasurable sense of horror I heard my husband drop into the silence the startling news that we too were in the market and should be grateful if the Rusts would kindly show us round the premises. As we tiptoed up the stairs in the wake of our guides I saw Gordon's glazed expression and knew that he was no less shaken than I at what he had got us into.

We didn't really possess the necessary qualifications for viewing a house at all; we saw that later. From some deep recess of my mind I dredged up an item of advice from an article I'd once read on the subject—something about cornices. One had to check them for something or other but I couldn't remember what it was. At the same time I was frantically doing mental arithmetic involving selling prices and mortgages and always coming up with the indisputable answer that in actual hard cash we had just about enough to cover a wire to America.

One thing, the house didn't *have* cornices—no ceilings to speak of, either: all the rooms except the kitchen were open to the rafters. It seemed rude to poke for woodworm or dry rot

11

when Mr Rust repeatedly promised us that we should have a good house if we bought it, though when he and his wife stopped by the door of the sitting room so that we could only peer into the furniture-filled gloom between their concave profiles, and Mrs Rust assured us that it wasn't damp we could smell, only honey, because it was in there that they pressed it, we really should have smelled something, if only a rat.

The next morning I shot off to break the news to my mother and to recommend that seventy-four was an ideal age to take up farming as a career. After a surprisingly short time, during which she sorted out which of us had taken leave of her senses, she stoically agreed to sell her house and come with us, and I returned home, where I attached myself to the telephone for the rest of the day.

Gordon, in the meantime, was occupied in pushing through heavy swing doors, walking endless corridors and stumbling up numerous flights of stairs as he tracked down vital people in the offices of solicitor, building society, house agent and bank. By the time he had penetrated the sanctum sanctorum of the bank manager and had been invited to sit down, he was so confused that he sank into the manager's own chair, which nonplussed them both for a moment. At least Gordon hadn't actually put his feet on the desk, so it could have been worse. All these people gave their attention to our problem — even the bank manager — but each shook his wise old head. 'Three days!' they cried, throwing up their hands. Three weeks, perhaps, but three months would be better.

That evening we paid a flying visit to Westwath. It was to be a leave taking of the farm, the bungalow, the beck. We drove back in moonlight on a tinsel ribbon thrown across the dark shoulder of the moor.

Wednesday crawled by in an agony of suspense. At eight o'clock we could bear it no longer and Gordon phoned Westwath to ask who were the lucky owners. To our astonishment, we learned that the Rusts still were; the bidding had not reached the reserve price and the sale had been abandoned.

Once more we were thrown into a turmoil. So much of a turmoil that I felt sick, though whether it was due to excitement or to being five months pregnant I couldn't be certain. The telephone practically steamed as we set machinery in motion again, keeping one hand on the brake just in case, because try as we would we could not pin the Rusts down to anything. Naturally they wanted the best price they could get and from someone with ready money, but we daren't put our house on the market until we were reasonably sure that Westwath was there for us to move into.

We were fast discovering that nailing Mr Rust was like trying to kneel on a balloon. He got out from under every time and discussed the weather in great detail, even to the farthest isobar. Then one day Mr Rust phoned to tell us that it was a lovely day there, though it had been foggy the day before, and he hoped it would be nice tomorrow. There was a bit of wind but it was sunny. I told him that it was very nice here, too, and I hoped it wouldn't rain. Just as I thought we were going on for the shipping forecast he asked us to tea the following Sunday 'to talk things over'.

Things finally began to move. Apparently all the other runners had either fallen by the wayside or turned out to be non-starters. Now we were the current favourites. Selling houses, the Rusts said wonderingly, was more trouble than they'd expected. It seemed funny as they'd had dozens of folks after it, and one man had offered thousands just for the fishing rights alone.

Well, we told them, we had *two* houses to sell. We could advertise mother's straight away, but we had begun alterations on ours before we'd had any notion of moving, and these would have to be completed or prospective purchasers might break a leg before ever they got up the drive.

Then Mr Rust came up with what seemed a splendid idea. With the proceeds from mother's house we could buy the farmhouse, the bungalow, garden, orchard and garage. We could then move in and Gordon could get a job to tide us over. There were plenty of jobs going, he said. Why, at the nearby RAF establishment civilians were getting twenty pounds just for sweeping up. In the meantime he, Mr Rust, would let the twelve and a half acres of land on a yearly basis — plenty would be glad of it — and he would give us first option at the end of the year which would give us plenty of time to settle all our affairs. It sounded marvellous.

That was the year the building societies suddenly tightened

their money bags and although there were many aspirants, it seemed an interminable time before mother signed her house over to someone else and came to live with us, despatching her furniture to Westwath to be stored in the bungalow. When it was our turn, the strain of keeping the house tidy made us all lose our appetites. Not that that was such a bad thing because, afraid as I was of being caught with greasy pans, I hardly dare cook anything and took to whipping plates from under my husband's nose before he had time to lay down his fork. People came, professed themselves delighted with the house, the garden, the view and the price, promised to return with mothers-in-law or stepsons and that was the last we saw of them.

One couple did return and their surveyor subjected us to the third degree. He managed, without speaking more than a dozen words, to reduce me to a quivering jelly. His narrowed, disillusioned eyes took the house apart. He rolled back the carpets and stamped on the floorboards, poked at the window frames and peered into cupboards. I've never seen anything so thorough in all my life. If he hadn't taken a firm grip on himself he would have climbed up the chimney, too. We awaited his report with dread and mentally reduced our asking price to a pale shadow of its former self. Eventually the letter came and our confidence was restored. He had not been able to find fault with the house and was so disappointed about it that to relieve his feelings he insisted that we straighten the ridge on the garage roof.

A few weeks later I opened the gate to Westwath — *our* gate to Westwath — and hopped back into the overloaded car which bumped on down the steep, rough track. Gordon drove particularly carefully so as not to waken three-months-old Roger, sleeping in his carry-cot among the cat baskets and sloshing goldfish tank, but I daren't look as we made the sharp right-angled turn onto the wath. It looked just wide enough for a pram and the beck was flowing very swiftly — I remembered that Mr Rust's weather reports had been unusually wet — but St Christopher gave us a shove and we drove through the farmyard and up to the garden gate with the goldfishes' high water mark barely lowered an inch. The Rusts were there to greet us and before you could say muck-spreading had sold us half a dozen hens. The new venture had begun.

2   What Time is the Next Bus Back?

'If tha wants owt doing tha'd best do it thisen' we read. We ought to have recognized the writing on the wall and gone back to civilization and plumbers before ever unloading so much as an egg-whisk. Instead, poor saps, we exchanged indulgent smiles at the whimsy of the rustic message on the plaster plaque which, abandoned by the Rusts, who no longer had need of such counsel, hung rakishly from a nail on the back hall wall. Legacies from the Rusts, such as this plaque and the fox's mask which snarled horribly from the opposite wall, turned up for years afterwards, the purpose of most of them being mystifyingly obscure.

It was in the teeth of this warning that Gordon abandoned his trusting wife and family to the almost empty house — some of mother's furniture was already in there rather gloomily holding the fort — and went off to waylay the pantechnicon should it happily chance upon the right road.

Bert and Ben, the removal men, had had a trying morning. Most of our furniture was too jaded to offer much resistance — seeing it standing there on the footpath you wouldn't have offered twopence for the lot — but the wardrobe, being younger and stronger, put up a good fight. They brought it out of the bedroom sideways, lengthways, endways, in a sort of wardrobe samba, but every time they were defeated by the bannisters. There was even dark talk of sawing it in half and precedents were quoted with morbid relish. Clutching a tin box containing stair carpet clips I bounded up the stairs to plead the wardrobe's case.

'It went *upstairs* all right,' I volunteered anxiously, and they agreed handsomely but ambiguously, I thought, to have

15

another bash. Like a music-hall turn retreating into the wings and bouncing back again with yet another funny hat, they would back into the bedroom and emerge once more in a different order, wardrobe predominating. The battering ram position looked set to be a winner. Bert was in the lead: right arm straight down by his side, head supporting the wardrobe, left arm smartly across his chest in a preparing to slope arms position, left hand and right ear pressed to the wardrobe door. I could understand the jaunty angle of his corduroy cap. It was reasonable that he should buffer his head against the hardness of the wood, but it was unfortunate that the angle became so acute that it blinkered his eyes, for the next minute his shuffling footsteps had closed with the stairclip tin which I had put down to clasp my hands in supplication. The noise and language were simply awful, but at least there was no more nonsense about the impossibility of geting the wardrobe downstairs.

Now Bert and Ben were having a trying afternoon. Taken a wrong turning, they had, adding a few unwanted miles. They'd nearly run into their own backboard on hairpin corners, had almost taken to the air over hump-backed bridges and expected to lose their roof under another, and here they were descending a one-in-four hill with the brake nearly through the floorboards and trying to round another bend without removing half a wall. . . when my husband *pounced* out on them and with frantic pantomime directed them into a hitherto hidden turning.

Gordon welcomed them matily. 'Ha! ha! You got here then!' he said. So it was not altogether surprising that they thought they had arrived, especially as there before them at the end of the cul-de-sac was a house. They stared at it and it stared blankly back at them. It resembled a child's drawing with a window pushing each corner, a door in the middle and the whole thing leaning cosily towards the hill. Actually the house was perpendicular and the hill leaned, but they weren't to know that. With a strange look at Gordon they slid out and went aft to let down the ramp.

'Bit remote, isn't it?' observed Ben gazing with wondering eyes at the windswept heather. The only other living creature in sight, a burnt-porridge-coloured sheep, bleated dolefully in

16

reply. Behind Ben the deserted road continued its precipitous way, shying sharply from a drunk and disorderly hurdle gate and plunging out of sight round the bend. The valley below appeared to consist of primeval forest and the whole was surrounded by dun-coloured moor. It was only when Bert, almost obliterated beneath a crate of books, began to stagger towards the house that Gordon tumbled to the mistake.

With another hearty laugh he pointed it out to them. He was sorry, he must have confused them about the house. This wasn't it.

'No?' said Ben looking around warily for the mouth of a cave. Considerately Gordon turned him round and indicated the inebriated hurdle gate and without a word the three of them walked down to it and peered over the top rail.

'There isn't a house down there?' said Bert in the fatalistic tone of one who knew there jolly well would be. What threatened to become an embarrassing situation was saved in the nick of time by the arrival of Joe with his tractor and trailer.

The materialization of Joe seemed like a miracle. Hitherto he had been just a name floating nebulously in and out of the Alice in Wonderland-type discussions we had had with the Rusts. By sheer perseverance we established that Joe was a neighbour's son who, we fervently hoped, had agreed to help with the last stage of our removal, so it was with unbounded joy that Gordon welcomed his appearance.

I am glad I was spared the agony of witnessing the further humiliation of our furniture. Stacked high on Joe's trailer, dipping and swaying like a palanquin, it groaned and rattled down to meet and breast the foaming wave because, by this time, the beck had risen and was several inches deep over the wath. It reminded him, Gordon said, of King John crossing the Wash and he preferred not to remember what happened to *his* goods and chattels.

Water, in one form or another, has been the chief contributory factor to this clump of grey hair limply overhanging my corrugated brow. Either there is too much of it when the beck gets too big for its boots and shows off all over the farmyard, or else there is none at all as we discover when the lavatory chain comes down with an empty, shoulder-dislocating thud.

On the third day in our new home the hot water system

17

turned temperamental. We turned on the tap but nothing came out. We spun it to its limit and heard an angry hiss as the hot water flounced back up the pipe. We knew it was up there somewhere because we could hear it growling and banging about. When appealed to, Mr Rust — characteristically, as we were beginning to find out — told us to leave it alone.

'It'll be all right,' he said, 'in a day or two. See?'

As it happened we had no alternative. There were too many more pressing problems to occupy our time. So we left it to sulk and went on playing solitaire with our furniture. Two days later we still had no hot water.

'Eee,' said Mr Rust wonderingly. 'Hasn't it come on yet? It should have done,' he went on severely. 'It has never been off as long as that before.'

Obviously we had not been chanting the right incantations or had been frittering away idle hours pushing marbles up the hot pipes. I was getting pretty desperate I can tell you, trying to bath three boys and wash acres of floor in a kettleful of water and I beat my breast, howling that something would have to be done.

At last Gordon, tired of pushing beds about in attics, waved aside Mr Rust's wait-and-see policy and got down to brass tacks. I wasn't sure that the cure wouldn't be worse than the complaint when I heard them discussing alarming practices like bleeding pipes, and I closed weary eyes to activities involving lengths of tubing and dismantling most of the airing cupboard. When Mr Rust had ambled placidly home for his tea, Gordon, becoming more and more frustrated with the way things were developing, said through clenched teeth that he didn't believe the fault was in the pipes at all, but in the tank in the attic. So when he got up there and proved himself right by removing the piece of bracken stalk which was blocking the inlet pipe, releasing the water with a choking cry into the cistern, you would have thought he would have been delighted. He wasn't.

He now discovered that the tank was half full of tomato sauce. He jammed the bracken stalk back into the pipe, scooped up a handful of the stuff and shone the torch on it. The gory substance gleamed dully in the torchlight and dripped thickly back into the cistern. I stifled a scream in my throat — after all the children were in bed — and climbed down from the rafters. Gordon was taking a closer look.

'Iron,' he said, 'out of the water. Can't have been cleaned out for years.'

Thankfully I prepared to descend the stairs. If that were all it was we could attend to it in the morning. But I reckoned without my indefatigable husband. 'Never put off until to-morrow . . .' he said smugly. 'We'll do it now.'

I stared at him in utter disbelief. It was well past midnight and for the last hour I had been wondering how I should summon enough strength to climb into bed. After a sleepless night with a baby who didn't know when he was well off, I had dragged, hoisted, scrubbed, cooked, washed, fed hens, cats, dogs, people, lambs; pushed, shoved and lifted until parts of me threatened to break loose and desert. Discord was creeping in but just as I was about to withdraw my ambassadors the torch went out and I was unceremoniously despatched below for an oil lamp and a couple of buckets.

As deftly as an ice cream man Gordon slapped gobs of the syrupy iron into a pail, expertly wiping his hand round the rim to foil the escaping rivulets. I rather fancied that part of the job myself, but my task as third labourer was to take the brimming pail and stumble down the steep uncarpeted attic stairs, hurting myself as quietly as possible. I had to feel my way down the unlit staircase to the ground floor, outside into the dark, wet and noisy night, there to tip the viscous stuff down the drain. It was like pushing treacle through a sieve. Actually, it looked just like red lead, and that night we disposed of enough to paint the Queen Elizabeth II from stem to stern, with plenty left over for the lifeboats.

Next morning Gordon showed the offending bracken fragment to Mr Rust. Aye, well, he thought it might have been something like that, he said casually. Likely the top tank was due for a clean. He had always scrubbed it out every year. No he hadn't, then, said Charlie Rawdon, on whose land our storage tank was sunk, when Mr Rust and Gordon, hung about with buckets, crowbars, a gavelock, a short ladder and a packed lunch went to scour it out.

This tank, Mr Rust explained to me in an expansive moment, collected and stored the water from our spring which rose somewhere in Charlie's field which lay up there above the top boundary of the forest. 'Up there' and 'down yonder' accompanied by an all-embracing wave of the hand was the closest Mr Rust ever got to concise directions and many a stray hiker vanished without trace after striving to follow them.

At teatime the men returned, rather muddy and dishevelled. He had been surprised, said Gordon, just how much silt had accumulated in a year. Well, it might have gone a bit longer, this time, said Mr Rust. But anyway, it would last now until next spring.

3   Shepherds of the Hills

It came as something of a surprise to find that the land and outbuildings had not been leased off as Mr Rust had so confidently predicted, and that the cows we recognized as holiday acquaintances were still in residence. What had become of all the eager beavers who had been clamouring for them we were not told, but that everything was still in Mr Rust's hands became obvious when, in the same breath in which he thanked us for the hen money, he asked if we wanted to buy the land. You could have knocked us down with an oxgang. We didn't have to be mathematicians to work out a mental sum of our assets: thirty three pounds and a house 'sold subject to contract'.

When the lights had stopped flashing and the bells had eased off a bit, we pointed out that it had been his own suggestion to let the land on a yearly basis, thereby giving us much more than the few weeks needed to settle the rest of our affairs. For answer he stared at a distant point over my left shoulder, drew his bushy white eyebrows together and frowned darkly.

The next day and on every alternate day thereafter we telephoned our solicitor or Mr Benson who, we hoped, was buying our house. They both made reassuring noises which we relayed to Mr Rust on intermediate days, when he asked us if we wanted to buy the land. Three months later the sale of our house was completed, we left the price of the farmland with our solicitor and with the rest bought the outbuildings, three cows, five calves and some of the sheep.

We hadn't intended taking the sheep at all. Sheep farming calls for special know-how and dedication far beyond anything that we had experienced, so we never considered it for a

21

minute, as we had told Mr Rust over tea that eventful Sunday. All right, he would sell them, said he; there were hoards of people clamouring for those too. If the presence of the cows was a surprise, the existence of the sheep came as a thump behind the ear. Not that we learned about them for some time. Unlike the cows, which grazed more or less in sight of the farmhouse, the sheep roamed the moor, intermingling to some extent with other flocks and kept at bay by strategically placed cattle grids.

Even the two pet lambs tethered to posts in the garden failed to warn us. The Rusts said that they thought we would like to keep them as an attraction for the children of holiday visitors and, no less attracted ourselves, we had gladly agreed. I suppose we presumed that they were left-overs from the dispersed flock, orphaned and too young to leave home.

Those two had me enslaved. No Eastern potentate was more cossetted. When I wasn't preparing bottles of warm milk I was moving their posts to new pastures. Time and time again I ran out to disentangle them from every hazard within their rope's radius and I spent ages cutting down leather belts to make collars which never lasted more than a couple of days. Whenever they broke their tethers they made a bee-line for the kitchen, clip-clopping about the concrete floor and poking their noses into cupboards. When the midday sun shone hot I moved the lambs into the shade of trees; if it rained I gathered one under each arm and ran with them to the shelter of their hut. I did this once while someone from the Ministry of Agriculture was sitting in the kitchen. When I returned he was glassy-eyed and speechless, and it was some time before he could find words to explain to me a few facts about sheep. We thought those two trying enough but we were still blissfully unaware of their relatives.

During those first few weeks I had no time to look beyond the garden and farmyard so saw nothing that went on outside their boundaries, but Gordon and the boys, clad in clinging macintoshes, did achieve a few short sorties out onto the moor, returning to drip into the baby's pram and regale me with heart warming stories of little lambs found dead in gulleys. After two or three of these trips and a mounting death toll Gordon mentioned his concern to Mr Rust.

'Aye,' he said absently, 'it's the wet that kills 'em. Have you rung Atki'son?' At least that's what it sounded like, but knowing no Atkinson and having no immediate desire to ring one, we thought we must be mistaken.

Next day Gordon reported more of the pathetic little corpses.

Mr Rust looked up abstractedly. 'Did you ring Atki'son?' he enquired of that mysterious being behind my left shoulder.

Somewhat taken aback I rather pettishly asked *what* Atkinson and Mr Rust, in an exasperated tone which implied that even I should know this, replied that if I hung a sack over the farm gate Atki'son would stop and collect. By this time I was certain that I was tuned in to the wrong programme and gave up trying, but over Gordon enlightenment dawned.

'Atkinson is a fellmonger?'

'Aye, that's right. Knacker. Have you rung him?'

We admitted that we hadn't, wondering what the crime of disposing of other people's fallen stock would be called and what the other people would do to us if we committed it. Mr Rust lost interest in the subject and drifted away, while we, having other matters to occupy us, let the rather odd incident slip from our minds.

I don't remember exactly when it was that we learned of the flock's existence but it was some time before that day when Gordon stood, cheque book in hand, before Mr Rust as he, licking his pencil, worked out how much sixty-one ewes with lamb at foot would be in good Fussey money.

Lamb at foot! Gordon and I exchanged sentimental glances, seeing in our mind's eye those dear little creatures trotting close by mother's protective side. We said of course we didn't mind them not actually being brought in for counting, Mr Rust being not well and all, even though they were to cost every penny we had and some we hadn't yet. Thus, very much to our surprise, we became sheep farmers.

I at any rate should have known better. When I was five years old and in the kindergarten I was once coerced into a white frock, all frills and embroidery, a pancake hat whipped up out of more frills and ribbons on my protesting head, and armed with a crook made from white rolled paper and tied with a ribbon bow. Then, as Little Bo-Peep, I was cast forth into the vast arena of the infant school's assembly hall to look for my truant sheep. Rehearsals were terrible. The little boys who were my lambs, when exhorted to gamble ('Lightly, Denis, *lightly!*'), thundered across the floor on all fours like charging bison, lost their sheepskin rugs and broke my crook. On the big day I wandered about on my allotted course, mortified by my now weak-necked crook, conscious that the eyes of the world were upon me, and that whatever the future held in store it would not be a glorious career on the stage. At last, in full view of the audience and to the delight of that *horrid* Denis, I burst into tears and wept silently while the 'chorus off' recited the whole of that interminable drama. I should have recognized it as an omen and had more sense than to dabble with sheep again.

And so, for that matter, ought Gordon, after his fiasco with the pet lambs.

Though their care was largely my headache, Gordon did contribute to their welfare by feeding them with their last bottle and putting them to bed. He would collect the warm milk from the kitchen, release the lambs from their collars and lead the way down the yard to their night hut. The little dears would first skip up to the kitchen door to call goodnight, then race off after Gordon, bouncing around his legs like new tennis balls. Gordon would beam at them affectionately saying wasn't it wonderful how they had taken to him? I could have told him they were more taken with the bottles they knew they would get once inside their hut. They were so taken with those that they were still hanging onto the teats when Gordon shut the door, wiping them off like paint from a brush.

Nevertheless, Gordon was convinced that it was his instinctive good shepherding so when someone reported that some sheep had strayed onto the road and would Mr Fussey mind putting them back on the moor, he was delighted. Bloated with pride he called authoritatively to the two sheep-dogs lying in the yard and strode purposefully across the wath and the garage field to the road. Confidently he refrained from looking over his shoulder, the obedient pattering of foot-steps at his heels confirming his recent but resolute belief in his vocation.

Good old sheepdogs, he thought sentimentally. Faithful,

intelligent, ever mindful of their master's needs. Their instinct to chase had been harnessed and shaped by generations of shepherds, like himself, for man's benefit so that a mere word, whistle or click of the tongue would send them like arrows from the bow to usher away, single out or gather the sheep to the fold . . . Musing thus, he opened the gate to the road and was feeling ever so slightly doubtful about which word, whistle or click of the tongue meant *get those damned sheep down from that steep bank opposite, off the road, up the hill and keep them by the gate next to the cattle grid, then send them through when I open it* when the problem was solved for him. Hoping to gain inspiration from the dogs themselves he turned to find, not man's faithful friends dutifully awaiting their master's commands but two tiny lambs, happy faces alight with anticipation, skittering round the gatepost at his heels.

Gordon returned home quietly, still tailed by his devoted followers. The dogs lay in the yard regarding the procession disinterestedly. Gordon stalked past, completely ignoring them, and when some time later I asked him if the sheep ever got back to the moor he replied, rather shortly, that he hadn't enquired. A surprising lack of interest, I thought, in one so dedicated.

4   *We Always Got Ours in Bottles*

In the meantime the cows, in the manner of their kind, went on producing milk, and the Rusts came morning and night to extract it. They set up HQ in a corrugated iron shed on the dividing boundary between farmyard and garden, which is now Gordon's workshop. Goodness knows what they had in there. Apart from the milk pails and sile there was a calor gas ring on which they brewed tea for themselves and syrup for the bees, banked on all sides with a heterogeneous collection of objects, removed from the house on their way to a doubtful fate.

The Rusts arrived early each morning, fresh after a good sleep unbroken by nocturnal baby recitals, and sniffed disapprovingly at us as we staggered outdoors, prising open muscle-bound fingers and asking each other what day it was. After milking they either held court in the shed or marched down to sit in the kitchen, the backwash of their passing waking the baby, who had only just relaxed threateningly gesticulating fists. There they would stare censoriously at our unshaken rugs and tell us of all the work they got through before breakfast while one or another of us sat with them out of civility and chafed at the time thus lost. One day, Mr Rust suggested that if we would take over evening milking it would save him the effort of turning out again. So began our first lesson.

My first thought as I stood on the threshold of the dimly lit cowhouse and gazed at the three enormous rumps looming horribly side by side was that I was a fool to have left Bellfield Avenue. Actually it was my only thought because after that my brain went numb. My legs weren't numb because I could feel them trembling and it was more to relieve them than anything, that I sat down on the three-legged stool muttering, 'We be of one blood ye and I,' in accents comprehensible to bovines, I hoped, I threw myself on Bluebell's mercy.

They had given me Bluebell because she was the oldest and most tolerant and, they said, easy to milk. She was short legged with an udder which barely cleared the ground and to reach it I had to press my cheek to the swell of her corporation which was black and looked like old railwayman's trousers that had seen earlier service lagging pipes. An Angus, they said she was. Certainly she was tolerant. She looked warily over her shoulder at my quaking form, turned up slightly bloodshot eyeballs, and after burping up a wad of cud chewed resignedly for the next hour. That was the length of time it took me to milk her.

Ten minutes of cautious squeezing and the pail was still as dry as the Sahara. Ten minutes more and the bottom of the bucket looked like a map of the Orkneys at low tide.

How was I doing, called Gordon cheerfully from his seat beside Rosie, next cow but one.

'Not very well,' I whispered modestly. I whispered because I didn't want to remind Bluebell that I was there, though as a matter of fact, as far as she was concerned, I wasn't. 'I don't think she's *got* any milk,' I went on hoarsely. 'There's not much coming out.'

The swishing noise in Gordon's pail stopped while he considered my remark. (It was an irregular swishing noise but at least it was recognizable as such, unlike my sporadic pinging.)

She must have, said Gordon at last. Old Rust had got a pailful last night. Couldn't I feel the flow of milk in the teats? As a matter of fact I could. I couldn't think why it should be going upwards. 'No,' I lied.

Gordon thought that very strange and suggested that I couldn't be doing it right. Was I giving a sort of squeeze and pull at the same time? Through clenched teeth and streams of perspiration I told him I was and he said in that case perhaps I should be doing it harder.

I brushed aside the hair which was plastered across my face, closed my eyes, held my breath and squeezed hard, cringing as I awaited the expected retaliatory kick. Bluebell chewed on without batting an eyelid. More confidently I returned to the attack. A thin white thread, so fine as to be almost invisible, streamed into the pail and the lagoons on the bottom of the bucket gradually enlarged and met to form an ocean. I laboured on, my saturated blouse sticking to shoulders that felt as if they'd been pierced with knives in several places. I fixed my sights on a dark mark in the zinc halfway up the pail. Imperceptibly the tide of milk crept upwards and covered it. I fixed on another mark a little higher. The pain in my hands, arms, shoulders, back and legs was excruciating. Sweat poured off in gallons and I was sure I should never be able to prise myself away from Bluebell's suffocating hide if the time ever came when I should be released. When the bucket was almost full the stream dried up.

'I've finished,' I said weakly.

Kind hands raised me to my feet and took the bucket from my nerveless grip. I shambled Quasimodo-like into the sunshine. But relief was short-lived. I had hardly savoured the joy of freedom when it hit me: I was going to have to go through it all again the next day. And the next, and probably for the rest of my life.

5   Gee, Thanks

The cows were not yet ours but milking time had suddenly become a milestone, a point by which our day was measured. Milestone was Gordon's word. Mine was millstone and it hung heavily about my neck. Every time I sat down beside those great beasts I felt I was taking my life in my hands. They were so *big*. Their bellies hung over me like the eaves of a house and sometimes they even rested them on me.

Bluebell at least stood still but Rhoda was addicted to Old Tyme Dancing and would slide, slide, slide, stamp, stamp until brought up by Rosie, and I slid, slid, slid my stool after her and backed again at the double as she went into reverse. Rosie was no dancer but she rolled like an old tub in a heavy swell, constantly changing her weight from one hind foot to the other without actually lifting them off the ground. She was inconsistent with her signals, too, often giving one blast for 'I am turning to port', and then going smartly astern carrying me into the dung channel with her. I called her S.S. *Rosie* and hoped she wouldn't sink *me*. Rosie had a way of holding back her milk so that we always had to pump for five minutes before she let it down, tiring us out before we started. There were about a thousand pulls to a gallon of milk.

Milking took such a slice out of our day that teatime became a matter of some importance and the subject of much discussion—either we had tea before milking when we weren't hungry, or afterwards when it ran into supper and we were so ravenous it ruined our budget. Eventually we settled for the earlier meal because we needed the scrap of evening which remained after the cows had swayed out to the night nursery in the back field, for working in the garden.

Daytime gardening was out because of the bees. We hadn't expected them to be living with us, either. They inhabited a motley array of Swiss chalets set in three rows: one across the bottom of the garden, one under the plum trees in the orchard and the third in the hay field at the top of the stone steps which led down to the garden.

They'd have to stay until back-end, declared Mr Rust. Couldn't move them while they were flying, could he? Put like that it sounded reasonable and besides we were obviously going to have to lump it. And we had better keep clear of the flight lines, he added severely, or we might get stung. It wasn't our skins he was worrying about, we knew that, but the consequent demise of the bees.

The sooner their demise the better so far as I was concerned because now, for the first time, I appreciated the true meaning of a bee-line. From thirty or so hives there was such a tangle of them that, had anything been distinguishable they would have resembled one of those pin and string pictures that are so fashionable nowadays. Where to put the baby's pram in safety became a problem requiring mathematical genius to solve.

Also because of the bees the Rusts were ever with us. It was worse than the mother-in-law problem. Go past the orchard to empty the ashes and a veiled head would appear over the wall and accuse me of taking the garden gate off its hinges. The wood was so rotten it had fallen off but telling him so earned me a stare of utter disbelief. It had never happened with *him*, he insisted meaningly. Go into the garden to hang out the washing and a voice from the hay field steps would point out that we'd dug up the foxgloves; didn't we like them, then? Considering that everything in the 'garden' that wasn't buttercups, nettles or old iron was foxgloves, I hadn't seen the harm in grubbing out half a dozen where I proposed to make a rock garden, but that, I was given to understand, was something that was not done here. Go down the yard to feed the hens and from the workshop where syrup was brewing amid an atmosphere thick with sorcery, a florid face would appear and demand to know why Gordon had taken the toolbox off the tractor? This I hadn't known about, but when I asked Gordon later, he gave me a funny look and explained that though the box had been lavishly equipped with a lid it hadn't run to anything so extravagant as a base, and lest someone should inadvertently drop tools inside he had thought it better removed altogether. Anyway, the tractor was our own property and what had it to do with the old — with Mr Rust, anyway?

The uncompromising truth was that everything was in a thoroughly run-down state just ripe for disintegration. When Gordon took apart the dilapidated old cart and hoisted part of it onto the workshop bench for repair, the bench collapsed in a cloud of sawdust. In sympathy an ancient bucket yoke dropped from the roof where it had been suspended for years and lay on the floor, a yoke-shaped heap of woodworm dust. Old Rust blamed us for that, too. None of these things had ever happened before, he complained in the manner of the man whose horse dropped dead between the shafts. Stoically, Gordon built a new workbench.

We incurred wrath if we hung a new gate or dug out a tree stump. What did we want to do that for? It had been all right for them.

Well, said Gordon one morning, he was wondering what to go out and do wrong first. What he actually did go out and do wrong was to stretch a length of barbed wire across the beck under the road bridge to stop the sheep getting in. It didn't stop the sheep and Gordon knew it wouldn't, but for weeks Mr Rust had been getting at me about it. He had always had a bit of wire across there, he said, and Gordon ought to have done the same.

What good would that do, asked Gordon irritably when I pestered him about it. I had no idea but was so fed up with being badgered I begged him to do it for my sake. So he did. It took all Sunday morning to hammer bolts between the stone courses of the bridge, float the wire across and make it fast. And the next day old Rust demanded to know what he'd done it for. A bit of wire warn't no good to stop sheep.

Then there was the business of the wasps. There were a number of wasps' nests about that summer and although they were of no inconvenience to us they were being troublesome to the bees, raiding the hives of honey and littering the ground around with casualties.

Gordon offered to burn them out with his blowlamp as he

31

had done before in our old garden with complete success. Mr Rust wouldn't hear of it. That warn't the way.

'Here,' he said knowingly, producing a nasty tin of something like algae-infested treacle. 'Put a bit of this inside the hole. That'ud settle 'em.'

What it was he didn't say and the label was ancient, filthy and illegible, but we supposed it was rat poison someone had given him about the year of Dunkirk. However virulent it had been then it had suffered an enervating process since, because although Gordon, under Mr Rust's watchful eye, put down enough to lay out a buffalo, the wasps ate it, waxed and grew fat and battered the bees worse than ever. This amazed old Rust. He thought Gordon was going to get rid of the wasps, he said.

Gordon had been putting down the poison regularly, I assured him earnestly, displaying the empty tin. That stuff, said Mr Rust derisively. That warn't no use. The knowing expression crept over his face again. Did Gordon have such a thing as a blowlamp . . .?

Then there was the problem of the rubbish. One way or another we had quite a lot of that, reinforced with the bungalow inhabitants' empty tins and bottles.

The dustmen never called here, Mr Rust had said. Why didn't we take it to the village and put it in the bin outside the post office? So every Friday when we visited the village shops we humped a paper cattle-food sack full of refuse into the boot of the car and self-consciously left it beside the post office bin. Sometimes we would be halfway to the village before we remembered and would have to go all the way back again.

By this time we had met and made friends with our neighbours, who owned the house in the inlet where our furniture van had unloaded. The Browns were not permanent residents so did not accumulate the amount of rubbish that we did, but what they did have they took over the moor to the tip. This was also on the advice of Mr Rust. He and Bertha, it seemed, often had a nice run out to the tip. Why he hadn't suggested that to us I don't know, but there we all were, the Browns having nice runs out to the tip when they would rather have been gardening, and we dumping embarrassing sacks in the village—until the week that Gordon took a job and was no more available for the Friday excursions. I was dubiously regarding a full dustbin one day when Mr Rust rolled up the garden path. When I posed our problem he looked blank. Why didn't we leave it by the road outside our garage? The dustman passed every alternate Wednesday, he said.

Funnily enough, the Rusts had never noticed the dilapidations at Westwath until we, driven to desperation, commented on them. Leaning on the white picket fence which curbed the greater celandine and nettles in the sliver of a front garden, the cheap distemper brushing off on his brown corduroys, Mr Rust would examine the house with a maudlin eye. Lovely bit of stonework, that was. We agreed that it was. We didn't get houses built like that nowadays. We agreed to that, too. There was nothing wrong with the way it had been built.

Well built, that was. He saw, he went on in the same breath, that Mrs So-and-so in the village had got such-and-such for her house. He paused meaningly and waited for us to comment. We didn't, but if we had it would have been to the effect that Mrs So-and-so's house had mains everything, including electricity, and had been well cared for, whereas ours had mains nothing and, we had soon discovered, woodworm, dry-rot, damp and an appalling lack of roof-tiles. The Bensons' surveyor would have been in his element.

The damp in the house was staggering and we couldn't smell honey for mushrooms. The lower four feet of the sitting room walls looked as if they were being submerged in a black wave. Friends entering the room unwarned were apt to reel back, crying out for the lifeboats. We couldn't invite them to sit there, for after ten minutes or so they would rise with their clothes clinging clammily to their bottoms and this caused embarrassment all round. After a few weeks the piano caught bronchitis and completely lost its voice, its woodgrain swelling up in goose pimples, and to this day I cannot run a duster over it without the cloth snagging as if on teazle burrs. The damp in the dining room was not so apparent, as the half below the chair rail had been lined beneath the wallpaper with wrapping paper, copies of *Woman's Own*, and the Church Magazines for 1967. They must have thought a lot of the Diocesan Leaflet as a damp course in those days, as Gordon remarked.

But all was not plain sailing at the Rusts' new residence, either. Their chimney still smoked a lot despite the cowl which they had removed from our chimney and taken with them, though, went on Mrs Rust happily, their roof was sound. At that particular time we were shovelling snow in our attic and bringing it downstairs in buckets. She blushed when I happened to mention it.

6   Where is thy Sting?

I didn't want to help with the bees. Not that I had anything
against them, mind you. In fact I had developed something of
a fellow feeling for them. Although they worked only a day
shift they more than made up for their evenings off and we
would exchange brief nods as they whizzed about their honey-
ing and I whisked out to lift the lambs down out of the sumach
and bring in the nappies. This mutual toleration lasted until
the day I was working in the hay field, breathing the scent of
drying grass, absorbing the warmth of the sun and thinking
pleasant thoughts, only vaguely conscious that somewhere in
the background a dynamo was humming.

I was concentrating on moulding the cocks into a pleasing
bun-shape, twisting my wrists professionally to make the last
swath fall in just the right manner to make a thatch, so it was
some time before the penny dropped. In fact only when the
bees were in my hair and stinging my neck did the illogical
sensation that I was somewhere in the vicinity of a ship's
engine room vanish like a pricked bubble and, like Pooh, I was
suddenly convinced that these were the wrong sort of bees. I
flung aside the hayfork and raced across the field leaping
cocks and windrows with adrenalin induced energy, pursued
by a blood-hungry mob thousands strong. I belted past the
row of hives gathering up flight lines like cobwebs and tumbled down the steps to the garden.

They were all in the kitchen, mother, Gordon, Mr Rust,
baby, pram and all with door and windows tightly shut against
the invaders. At first I thought they had even barricaded the
door when it only opened an inch and then stuck. Frantically I
beat on the wood and pleaded for admittance, feeling like a

benighted traveller arriving after curfew at York's Bootham Bar with wolves howling in the Forest of Galtres behind me. Then the pram which had been jamming the door shoved up and I tumbled inside.

There they all sat downing cups of tea, totally indifferent to my perilous plight, though as Gordon, using eyebrow tweezers, cheerfully removed the stings I was gratified to see Mr Rust's Santa Claus-like countenance registering concern. Had I, he enquired earnestly, resting his huge sandy-fuzzed hands on well-fleshed knees and leaning forward to catch my answer, noticed what colour the bees were?

I thought it was the most irrelevant question I had ever heard and no substitute for the sympathy I felt was my due, but he was going on to explain that he had three kinds of bees — I forget what they were called: Italian Blacks, Spanish Yellows and Mediterranean Blues, or something — and if only I'd had the presence of mind to stop and examine their jerseys he would have known which hive was causing the trouble.

I could tell him that anyway. It was the first one at the top of the steps. As I sped past I had seen the seething mass on the flight board elbowing for entry like shoppers at the January sales. A few eggers-on on the periphery, obviously professional agitators, actually left them to join my gang and were now bashing themselves silly on the window panes.

It turned out that that particular hive had carelessly lost its queen and had become so demoralized by the happening that a much stronger and more aggressive neighbour, commendably following the example of its human superiors, had marched over the frontier and laid siege. Raiding parties were plundering honey and carrying it back home and Number One hive was naturally in a tizz over it. My own contingent, riled at having nothing to sting, buzzed back to the battle-ground.

Thankfully, we threw open the door and windows and greedily gulped down air, then Mr Rust, calmly declaring that there was nothing he could do about it today, ambled contentedly off home.

The high pitched brain-deadening whine, like the background to a science fiction play, persisted until very late in the evening, union rules going completely by the board. Absolutely necessary outside chores were performed with one eye cocked heavenwards where desultory dog fights, reminiscent of the Battle of Britain, still went on. Odd detachments strafed us in passing but the main activity was centred on the captured hive where the victors caroused on nectar and honey until, praise be, they were too sozzled to hum any more.

As I said, I didn't want to help with the bees but occasionally I wasn't quick enough and the privilege was pressed upon me. My part consisted chiefly in handing things and being handed things and puffing smoke from a bellows charged with smouldering brown corrugated paper into the top of the hive. This gave the bees something else to think about while Mr Rust lifted the sections of comb. It also displeased them and once they had got over the coughing and wiped the tears from their eyes they would pick me out as the tormentor and give me what for. Squinting at a microscope's eye view of the honey bee as it zinged to and fro a mere inch from my nose with only a flimsy veil to keep us apart, I would take the brimming clammy cells from Mr Rust's steady, gloveless hands, carry them carefully into the house and cover them over with a sack. Sometimes this could go on for hours and on those days the family went without dinner.

Gordon wasn't keen to help with bees either but only because it took him away from rebuilding walls which seemed to have been down since Cromwell's time, digging out ditches to the original culverts six feet below, repairing fences and attending to the livestock. I laughed myself silly the first time I saw Gordon in bee-keeping outfit. He wore an old gabardine macintosh which he had bought years ago when length and square shoulders were haute couture. This came down well over his wellingtons. That, and a wide-brimmed hat, like the old scout type, swathed in black veiling, plus a pair of bright blue rubber gloves was a sight to bring people to a shuddering standstill. The baker's boy—a nervous type—almost fainted when, returning past the orchard with an empty basket, he first saw Mr Rust's bee-clouded head appearing over the wall, followed by The Man in Black apparition of my husband's. He took to his heels and didn't look back until he was halfway over the footbridge.

Poor Gordon. It turned out that he was allergic to bee

37

stings, which was a pity because he actually liked the creatures and had intended to keep a few hives of his own, but after several limbs had swollen up like balloons and his temperature had risen to sugar boiling point, he had reluctantly admitted defeat. From time to time we were compensated by the largess of a comb of honey, and this and rhubarb pie formed our staple diet for a few months.

Bee stings hardly troubled me but the midges did. Plodding through our garden with a barrowload of supers, Mr Rust demanded to know why we hadn't scythed them nettles down. He had always done it twice a year. We wanted them out, not down but knew it was useless to mention it. We could just hear him saying that there'd always been nettles at Westwath and didn't we like them, then? So we held our tongues, waited until evening then sallied out with spades and forks and began our campaign against the matted yellow roots.

The midges went hysterical with joy. For generations they had been yawning through their humdrum lifecycles, blunting probosces on cowhide, feeling that life had nothing more to offer when, bingo, mother, Gordon and I entered their orbit. There were we three, innocently bending our workworn backs to the task, rejoicing in the absence of bees, enjoying the out-pourings of a thrush at the top of the spruce tree while close by rhododendrons dripped scoops of strawberry ice cream into the evening sky-tinted stream, when the itching began. Nothing much at first, a mere irritation of eyelid and ear promptly forgotten during the interval while the scouts flew off to carry the glad tidings to the rest of the gang at Riverside Mansions. Then it began in earnest. From the yo-heave-ho step of the hornpipe as we hauled at nettle roots, the tempo changed through rumba rhythm as we scratched our backs against our shirts, to culminate at the Indian war dance as, trying to reach less accessible parts of our anatomies we hopped from one foot to the other, slapping frantically.

Night after night we went through the same routine. Swathed in scarves we peered out under puffy eyelids at the wilderness still to be tamed. Soaked in TCP, Dettol and vine-gar we repelled each other but not the midges. They loved us, with or without condiments. There had been no time to go shopping for trousers and my legs were putteed up to the thigh with bandages to protect the flesh I had scratched raw and to hide the infinitesimal scraps of still-whole skin from the enemy. It was while sweltering in this costume, bandages, scarves, balaclava helmet heavily garnished with mint, and smelling distinctly of pickles, that I met our local policeman for the first time. Remaining calm in the true tradition of the force, though undoubtedly making a mental note to check with the nearest loony-bin, he signed the animal movement book with a steady hand and informed us cheerfully and un-necessarily that the midges at Westwath had three pairs of jaws.

7   In at the Deep End

There is a witch cross incised in the stone doorway of our cow-house, a relic of the not so far-off days when witches were rife in our village. How the simple peasantry could be so gullible as to believe that cutting a cross in a doorway would keep out witches I cannot understand. Because it doesn't; they still get in.

Witch crosses and witch posts are still fairly common on the North Yorkshire Moors and create a certain amount of interest so I was not inordinately startled when one dark night Gordon peered round the back door, beckoned me to follow him and strode soft-footed down the garden path muttering darkly about witches and broomsticks.

It was a balmy evening. From the forest wafted waves of aftershave lotion and garlic and the flowers on the sycamore trees smelt like a brewery. The moon was just rising; piercing the gaps in the dry stone wall edging the top field. In silhouette, the wall looked like knotty crochetwork. Apart from the night-accentuated gurgle and splash of water and an owl giving a very good imitation of somebody imitating an owl, the night was silent. Gordon stood there as if moonstruck, one hand to an ear in a classical listening attitude. I stood beside him and gawped.

Suddenly there came the weirdest whirring sound and something swooped low over our heads. We both did an involuntary knees-bend followed immediately by another as the thing wheeled and whirred back again. With eyes like saucers we raked the sky while the uncanny thrumming swelled and faded again and again. We couldn't think what it could be — UFOs were seriously considered, outsize dragonflies tentatively thought of, but we both agreed that broom-mounted witches was really the most credible solution. The matter thus settled we leaned contentedly for a while over the handrail of the footbridge and watched the moon turn the beck to molten pewter.

A day or two later, as I was chatting to my advisers, the roadmen, I mentioned the intriguing sound. They doubted it were witches, they said thoughtfully. 'Could be snipe, though,' said Derek. 'Make that noise with their tails,' said Arnold. 'Drumming sound. Queer like.' They were right, of course, as I discovered when I looked it up.

As a matter of fact Derek is something of a bird man. His speciality is imitating the cuckoo and, in unlikely months such as February or November when there are strangers in the vicinity, he is wont to let off a few notes and gaze intently into a tree. He gets everyone staring searchingly into bare branches then moves on until there are little groups of retired teachers and colonels, and rucksack-burdened walkers dotted all over the village peering into bushes and later writing to the papers about it.

The roadmen identified another birdcall for me. Sometime earlier, Robert, our eldest (then nine years old and even at that early age capillaried with petrol rather than blood: unless a thing is made up of piston rings and crankshafts he isn't aware of its existence) and I were barrowing weeds to the compost heap when I heard such a splendid sound that I stopped dead in my tracks. It started on a low note and gradually rose in pitch and crescendo until it actually bubbled like an overfull whistling kettle. I noticed something resembling a seagull soaring afar off, but I had never heard a seagull do that before.

'Listen, Robert,' I said. 'Whatever can that be?' Robert's expression was as enthralled as my own.

'It's a muck-spreader,' he cried joyously, listening intently to an entirely different sound. And although the roadmen identified it for me as the curlew's spring song, to us it will ever be the greater muck-spreader's.

The roadmen worked on our stretch a lot that first year, luckily for me. They were ever ready to lend an ear to my problems, and, boy, did I have problems. When the summer season drew to a close and the last bungalow tenants departed,

41

taking with them our only immediate source of income, Gordon was compelled to go out to work in order to keep all our four-footed dependents in the manner to which they had become accustomed, and I was upgraded to farmer on the spot.

That Gordon would take a job had been the idea from the start, of course, but we'd imagined it would be a part-time one so that he could keep his eye on the farm. It did not work out like that. The RAF establishment was apparently bursting at the seams with sweepers-up and the nearest town had nothing better to offer than the post of part-time boilerman in a laundry at four pounds a week, which wouldn't have kept Bluebell in dairy nuts, so Gordon returned to full time employment in his old trade at a garage thirty miles away to the north.

Now, getting out early in the morning to attend to livestock was not entirely new to me. Back in Hull in wintertime I had often gone outside at the crack of eight in the morning to shake snow off the bluetits' nuts and to melt ice on the fishpool but these were tasks with which I was confident I could cope. About this new venture I was not so sanguine.

To begin with we got up at five thirty. Gordon wanted to allow himself ample time for the journey and I knew that however early I started I wouldn't get everything done.

'Sure you'll be all right?' said Gordon anxiously as he prepared to depart that first morning.

'No,' I replied, truthful to the last, steadfastly uncheered by his assurances that he would get home as soon as possible. Anything might happen before then.

I milked Bluebell and Rosie for the first time on my own, and let the little Angus and Hereford out of the calf pen and into the cowhouse to suckle Rhoda, confident that I should not get them back again. However, Robert and Antony, who were just leaving for school, helped to steer them in and, thankfully, I shot the bolt and leaned against the door, desolately watching the two small boys depart in the school taxi.

Not that I was entirely alone. Mother was indoors washing the dairy utensils and there was Roger, the baby, to be cared for. Once Roger was settled in his pram and the necessary chores — like sweeping cornflakes and straw out of the kitchen — were done, I hurried outside again to muck out the

42

cowhouse. The first time I did the mucking-out I felt definitely under-privileged but soon discovered that it wasn't such a disagreeable job after all. Indeed, thinking in terms of manure for my garden it became a positive pleasure.

I was hardly ever indoors after that so housewifely activities went by the board. Luckily visitors were thinning out as the days shortened so there were few to criticize. Those that did still venture I tried to keep outside as the farmyard was considerably tidier than the living room. Besides, it was much more interesting out there. Lambkin was growing up (the other little lamb had died) but was still a pet. The chicks we had known from the egg were now beyond the cute stage, having grown leggy and prickled with quills but the ducklings still bowled everyone over.

It had taken no time at all for a set of nine-year-old twins in Robert's form at school to convince me that all the best farmers were rearing Khaki Campbells and to sell me a dozen day-old ducklings, which we christened the Peepy Quacklings in our nauseating townee way. The twins' dad aided and abetted them by lending us a rearing box warmed by two oil heaters which I was convinced would roast them prematurely if I didn't check them every five minutes or so.

What with these and the hens, cows, calves, stirks, sheep and cats, not to mention mother and Roger, I was not what you could call lonely. And then there was Jess, the sheepdog.

Jess was another of the established inhabitants that we had encountered on our first holiday visit. She was then very young, barely out of the puppy stage and all squirms and laughter. In successive years we had watched her with her mother working among the sheep, very much the subordinate, an apprentice to a craftsman. Both dogs were still at Westwath when we moved there but Mr Rust took the elder into retirement with him and left Jess to become part of our hearts and lives. She has come to mean so much to us that we cannot imagine life without her. She took to all of us from the word go, probably because we advanced her quarters from a chain in the yard to a rug in the kitchen, although she still slept in an outbuilding (predictably known as the dog house) at night. She even accepted the cats, whom she tolerated with a sort of wonderment as they rubbed their arched backs affectionately

43

under her chin. She loved us all to distraction but chose me to cleave unto as long as we both shall live, and although she would obey any of the others so long as I was not in the vicinity, as soon as I hove in sight her attention and deference were transferred to me. This was aggravating for Gordon when he was doing something with sheep and an awesome responsibility for me.

Never had my true worth been recognized and so revered until I met up with Jess. She dwelt upon my every word, action and, I have no doubt, facial expression. A kind word from me as she sat and gazed raptly in my direction set her shuffling across the floor on her bottom like a baby on a potty, then she would butt my arm with a determined nose until I was forced to fondle her. I just had to remember not to smile at her while drinking anything, as many a cup of hot tea has poured into my lap during these paroxysms of love. I seldom uttered a sharp word because I couldn't bear the guilt I suffered at the sight of the dejection it brought on. Her entire body would droop, every hair wilting visibly, head hanging limply, the epitome of misery and despair. This Eeyore attitude was a big thing with Jess. She stood like that, nose just clearing the floor, if her name was not brought into the conversation every five minutes: Jess, Jessica, Jessica-panda, Dog, JESS spelt out, DOG or DO double-Dog. She also wilted thus over her bowls of luxury-class dog meat, offal, meaty bones and milk warm from the cow. That she should be expected to eat *this*. But she knew her place, she sighed sadly, and supposed she mustn't grumble. The second we turned our backs the dishes were empty.

. If she loved us, everybody (except the baker's boy) loved her. She must be the most photographed non-Crufts dog in the country, figuring prominently on holiday snaps taken by every visitor to our bungalow during the last eight years. She looks just like a panda, they tell us, originally. She does, too, long haired, black and white with a piratical patch over one eye.

To the baker's boy who, as I've mentioned before, was of a nervous disposition, the panda aspect was less evident than the piratical. Because she always barked to warn us of invaders Bernard was convinced that he would be torn limb from limb and hovered on the footbridge calling quaveringly that he was there, and was Jess fastened up? Because we always chained her when Bernard was due Jess took a dislike to him and barked worse than ever, and instead of desisting when he had come forward and declared himself as she did with anyone else, she kept up the cacophony until he had scuttled back to his van and slammed the door. In attempting to reassure him and to disclaim ill-will in Jess, mother and I rather overdid our apologies and explanations. After all Bernard was the only person who felt that way about her and we had a strong suspicion that he once had clouted her with his basket, an act guaranteed to offend her in the first place.

Jess was a mistress of disguises. She could transform her pirate face from Black Jake to Red Rover in a matter of seconds merely by digging out delicious smells from the tawny sand of the riverbank. Once she confounded a new postman by appearing auburn-haired and lugging a defunct rabbit one minute, and the next reappearing carrying a dead mole and with her whole face blackened with mole-hill earth, looking more like Funf than you would have believed possible. The mole, we were meant to understand, was supposed to be a bomb. One of those round ones with smouldering fuses.

She knows about these things, I suppose, because of her visits to the library. The library is a mobile one which comes to Westwath on alternate Wednesdays, turning cumbrously to park in front of the Browns' house. Usually I am its sole customer unless the boys are home from school or Binnie and Steven are in residence, and my allotted quarter of an hour is sheer bliss. Jess feels the same way, though her reasons have more to do with the titbits that the librarians are likely to produce, and the sight of me packing books into the basket sets her dancing with anticipation. She gallops up to the bridge, propelled by a madly spinning tail, lopes up the steps and stops dead on the narrow footwalk, waiting for me to catch up so she can take her place at my heel. She always does this, and sometimes we are accompanied by friends who, out of courtesy, I have ushered ahead; they find the bridge stoppered with dog and climb over it and each other in a welter of confusion because Jess won't budge until I get there. I find this rather touching but Binnie says that Jess's idea is that if the bridge is going to collapse, then she won't be on it!

8   'But Milk my Ewes and Weep'

The greatest time-consumers and our biggest headache were the sheep. They anguished my soul even more surely than did those in the infants' school so many years before. My costume was vastly different from those days, though, and neither did it bear any resemblance whatsoever to that of the Dresden china shepherdesses who simper expensively in protective glass cabinets. Muddy jeans thrust into rubber boots are a far enough cry from panniered satins but when one boot is the normal wellington length and black while the other barely covers the ankle and is brown (this because their true mates have sprung leaks) the wearer is apt to make a distinctive figure. Bo-Peep's white frills and embroidery were replaced by a once green jacket which, owing to the desertion of its buttons, cloth backing and all, was held together round the waist by a fraying length of Charley Turner (our usual name for binder-twine being, I believe, the name of a manufacturer of it).

The first time I met one of our neighbours, Charlie Rawdon as a matter of fact, he was wearing a similar jacket only its lining was hanging down in rags as well. I had mistaken him for a gipsy at first, and then, after being introduced, pitied him for his poverty which appeared to have been going on longer than ours. It was only later I understood. Friends are constantly showering cast-off jackets on me and I go through them like a box of paper hankies. Admittedly I'm the type who can't paint a window sill without the stuff dripping off my elbows or write a reason-for-absence note to school without getting ink on the back of both ears so my poor clothes hadn't a chance against animal horns, jagged bits of fencing and barbed wire.

One thing hadn't changed from infant school days, though. I still wrung my hands and wept. I'd had no idea that any creature could require so much attention, be prone to so many ailments, be so human, so lovable and so capable of utter unadulterated devilry as those four-footed woolly jumpers. We had thought that old Rust was shooting a line when he said that he recognized most of the flock individually but familiarity with them proved otherwise. We discovered that they all looked exactly like our friends and relations. There was Christine, named after our young neighbour in Hull. They were identical even to the hairband. There was Jean, Rene, Mrs Grassby and Mother-in-law. There was Cattle grid, so called because she came to meet me each morning crossing the grid on hands and knees. There was Daisy-May, the cutest thing you ever saw, looking just like a youthful Madam Pompadour. She had a little white beauty-patch on each black cheek, knife-edged ankles terminating in the tiniest polished black shoes and from the rear—the aspect most familiar to us as we chased her out of somewhere or other, tiny footprints like neat quotation marks ticker-taping out behind her—her skirts stuck out like panniers and flounced haughtily as she tit-tupped along. There was Maisy-Day, a plebeian edition of Daisy-May, and still with a French flavour there was even a set that looked hand picked for the scene around the guillotine, a slatternly lot with wool like cold mutton stew full of lumps of greasy potato. If they weren't actually knitting shrouds and their teeth weren't really blacked out they managed to convey the impression that they were. And not one of them, not Daisy-May, nor Cattle grid, nor even the infirm and half-blind ones and certainly not Christine and her bosom friend (whom we called Friend, though certainly she was no chum of ours) could be remotely described as sheepish, quiet as an old sheep or gentle as a lamb. They were all without exception she-devils incarnate.

I don't know how many times they stood like girls in senior assembly smiling politely at me as I encouraged them to play the game for the good of the flock and not to go out of bounds.

They listened with respectful attention while I exhorted them to refrain from climbing walls and crossing the cattle grid. Their expression was courteous in the extreme as I pleaded with tears in my eyes that they should not, please, please, go up the road to Castle Farm. Then the minute I dismissed them there they were shinning up and over walls like cats or pelting up the road to have illicit love affairs with the handsome tups at Castle Farm, St Trinian material to a man.

What with dosing, injecting, castrating, shearing, dipping and marking—that is ear clipping, horn-burning with Gordon's initials and rudding—they kept us constantly on the go, and as all this had to be done at the weekends when Gordon was home I spent days traipsing the moor with Jess, searching for our sheep, the ones with the red mark on their rumps.

Our sheep did not have the monopoly of that stretch of moorland. They shared it with Mr Anderson's, who were distinguished by their blue rears, and there were usually a number of others which had worked their way down from adjoining strays, or heafs, as they are called in these parts. Those marked with red on their right side belonged to Mr Stewart, Joe's dad, and red-necked ones were Harold Robson's. The blue-bottoms were thick upon the ground and I never ceased to wonder at the way they separated from ours as Jess ran among them. The long ribbon of road which led to the head of the valley acted as a dividing line, Mr Anderson's peeling off to one side, ours to the other.

They trickled downhill in twos and threes, joining up with others to form streams, the streams converging until a river of sheep was flowing steadily through the heather on a homing route taken instinctively by generations for perhaps hundreds of years. The sheep crossed the main road above the cattle grid and surged into the top field by way of the blasted gates.

Gathering would operate as efficiently as that when there wasn't an onlooker within miles but on days when cars parked by the dozen on the sheep-nibbled grass of the roadside while their occupants admired the scenery and emptied their rubbish all over it, the river of sheep would change its course right in the teeth of the yawning gateway, wheel smartly to the right and disintegrate along the Scar where they traversed its sheer rock face like lizards and thumbed their noses at Jess and me.

Then we would have to start all over again and this time most of the flock would run into the field — though only to see if the grass was greener there, then while we were off after the others they would decide that it wasn't and jump over the wall at the field's lower end onto the road, setting off up it for Castle Farm. They always made for Castle Farm as if sucked up there in a slipstream. Needless to say, Castle Farm is at the top of a one-in-four hill. All hills (which are rather sneakily called banks in order to faze the stranger) in our district are one-in-four with the exception of those which are one-in-three, and they all have hairpin bends in the middle and a river at the bottom. Anyway, I would plod up the hill towards Castle Farm just in time to see the last woolly behind disappearing into the forest, and as I helplessly stood there glancing despairingly back across the Scar towards our top field I would witness the collapse of the blasted gates and the exodus of the rest of the flock.

One day Jess was bringing a dozen defaulters down the bank as a carefree family party in a grey Mini drove unsuspectingly over the bridge on the bend at the bottom. They passed me on their way up, as happy as could be, mouths agape with laughter. One of them even waved to me. A few seconds later they passed me again as they came down backwards with a stalled engine. Their mouths were still open but their expressions had changed so radically that you would hardly have known them. They were completely surrounded by sheep, and Jess, recognizing it as a situation with possibilities, lay down on the crown of the road and watched with interest. As for me, I assayed a friendly wave, felt the moment was past and grimaced to register concern, sympathy, disbelief and, like Pooh Bah, disassociation to the point of not being there.

Those pesky sheep were always involving me in such incidents and during the high-spot of the pantomime somebody would drive past with uplifted hand and it was no use my looking nonchalant in the hope that they would take me for an innocent bystander because, for some reason, everyone seemed to know me. When I was first introduced to Mrs Stewart she gave me a very odd look and said, yes, she thought she'd seen

49

me with the sheep. She knew darn well she had, of course. Odd boots and all.

Then came November and tupping time. Now even I knew that in order to have little woolly lambs a ram would have to be involved sometime, but just when the nuptials were supposed to take place I hadn't the faintest idea and thought the subject too indelicate to consult the roadmen. So the first I knew about it was one day when old Rust stomped in and said why hadn't I got the yowes in and where was our tup? Considering that there had hardly been a day during the past six months when he hadn't been somewhere on the premises, and he knew perfectly well that we had never had a tup, I felt he might have spoken about it earlier.

However it provided him with an opportunity to make a great business of ringing up the neighbours to try to buy, beg or borrow a ram of some description. At this late hour it wasn't easy but at last a promise was made of a tup 'a bit au'd but still useful' by a farmer some distance away.

The tup was delivered one Friday teatime. I was just raising a cup to my lips when torchlight shone suddenly through the window accompanied by a sharp rap on the pane.

There stood Mr Watson, one of our wealthier farmers, with a few thousand acres of reclaimed moorland to his credit, wearing the raggedest, filthiest, most Charley Turner-girded macintosh that I had ever seen in my life.

'Got the tup,' he said. 'Where do you want it?'

We put it in the garage, which was the only Castle Farm-proof place I could think of on the spur of the moment.

'He's a bit au'd,' said Mr Watson carefully. He had only cost a fiver so I thought he might be. 'But,' he continued reassuringly, 'he's a good worker.'

I gulped and nodded, grateful for the darkness, being still innocent of all the X-certificate activities which take place on a farm. When he asked me how many ewes we had and I answered, 'Sixty-one,' I thought he looked slightly stunned.

'Well,' he offered handsomely after the briefest of pauses, 'if you get stuck give us a ring and I'll lend you a shearling.'

I would have found this more encouraging if he hadn't added, 'I reckon he's old enough,' as an afterthought.

When Mr Watson had gone I found a bit of chalk and wrote

in large letters on the garage door, TUP INSIDE to warn Gordon when he returned from work. Needless to say, he didn't notice it and by and by experienced a nasty shock.

The following morning we examined the new crew member by daylight. He was greatly displeased with his night's lodging and none too enchanted with us. Also he was a little older than I had thought. One of his horns, which curled extravagantly over a wicked yellow eye, finished its spiral in the flesh of his brow and had made rather a mess of it. His wool was like that of some of the tatty old harridans of our flock but was highlighted by a green rudd mark on one side. However it was the other side of his coat which drew us to gather round in wonder. It looked exactly as if a hot flat-iron had been left on him to burn right through. How he had achieved that tonsorial artistry we couldn't imagine.

After his horn and hooves had been trimmed and his head doctored up he looked a little more presentable, so we put him in the top field and gathered in the flock. All of it. Only at this point did we discover that although we had the full quota of sixty-one ewes, plus half a dozen old crones which must have escaped marketing for years by playing Robin Hood and his Merry Men in the forest, there were only seventeen lambs. So was solved the little dead lambs on the moor mystery; buying a flock uncounted was something else we kicked ourselves for.

Old Rust stood in the road and stared intently up at the sheep, apparently not noticing the discrepancy.

'Just to see if he's working,' he said placidly.

Actually the whole lot, Don Juan included, had their heads to the ground nibbling for all they were worth. They weren't acting like newly-weds at all.

'Bit o' good grass,' said their late owner and advised us to put them out onto the moor every night to make it last. Eventually the Hope of Westwath did venture to claim his marital rights, and Mr Rust went home satisfied.

We weren't nearly so happy though and as Jess sent them out onto the moor that evening, wiping round the sides of the field to gather up the stragglers, we seriously considered asking Mr Watson for the loan of the shearling; only the recollection of his expression convinced me of the futility of that.

Next day they were all clamouring to be let in again. That is all except the tup who we found way up the moor legging it back home as fast as he could. Quieter there, he said. Not so demanding. On the following day he was there, all right, but only twenty-four of the ewes were, the others having gone to look for some place with more action. But there they made a big mistake because having sweated the gate up in place and secured the cat's cradle of binder twine I discovered that I had collected somebody else's tup as well. I couldn't recall having actually heard of anyone in our village being lynched for rustling but there's always a first time and anything going on in that top field of ours is very visible to anyone passing on the road below. And, believe me, there were quite a lot of goings-on in the vicinity of that young and handsome ram.

In our efforts to separate him out Jess and I were surrounded by a jostling mob of besotted females shrieking that if he went they were going, too; most of them did, so we spent the next hour or so scouring the district again. Honestly, I despaired of ever getting them all legally wed. Each day for a fortnight Jess and I combed the moor for defaulters, turned them into the field with our blessing and left them to fate and our tup. Until the day he disappeared.

On the previous evening he had ambled out with the rest, an elderly gentleman seemingly content with his lot. One could almost see the pipe and carpet slippers and imagine him just managing a short turn round the garden before settling for the night . . . and the next morning he had gone and was never seen again. Not by us, our neighbours or Mr Watson whom we phoned in case the old man had had an urge to revisit the scene of his lambhood. Green mark, red mark, flat-iron brand and all had vanished like the Cheshire cat.

Privately, I rubbed my hands in glee and breathed a sigh of relief. That was the end of that. No more trudging these high wide hills and rough uneven ways. I could now stay at home and mend pillow cases. And that's just where I was wrong because the next day it snowed.

9 'And Dick the Shepherd Blows his Nail'

It had been freezing hard for days. Even the normally restless beck had been forced into a straitjacket of ice, a single rivulet threading a twisting cord through the floes. 'Sky's full of snow,' said everyone wisely. 'It'll be warmer when it comes.'

It was on a Saturday when it did, I remember. We had planned to go Christmas shopping—we still planned things in those days. Anyway, it was the first snow we had experienced here, Gordon was home and we were going to enjoy it. There was no need to search for sheep this morning. They were all gathered around the cattle grid doing their celebrated imitation of Percy Edwards as we floundered up the hill dragging a sledge invisible beneath an enormous sack of hay. All, that is, with the exception of Lambkin who, ever since he had been promoted from the garden to the Top field, had remained aloof from the common flock. He still occupied the field in solitary splendour, finding it incredible that we should expect him to go out onto that draughty moor with the rank and file.

He was the cause of great embarrassment to Jess. The first time she had attempted to round him up with the others she had been close on the heels of the fleeing flock and had run full tilt into his immovable bottom. They had both crumpled up like concertinas. Nonplussed, Jess turned to me for instructions and sympathy. Lambkin flung her an astonished look, shrugged his shoulders and resumed his interrupted lunch, utterly disassociating himself from her and the rest of his own kind. So the situation continued, Lambkin going his own sweet way, oblivious to the others though still devoted to me, and the cause all too often of trouble with the blasted gates; Jess ever afterwards gave him a wide berth, averting her eyes and pretending she couldn't see him.

He reckoned nowt to the snow and complained bitterly to us through the bars of the lower gate. We'd had to put netting over the gate because during the first few days of his exile he had squeezed between the bars, regularly turning up at the kitchen door pleased as Punch with himself. He received his ration of hay grumpily and turned his back on us to eat it. It was a different story at the cattle grid. Les Citoyens Français had back-tracked into an earlier scene and were rioting and screaming out for bread. There the strongest triumphed and the weak (us) went under.

We escaped to the safety of Lambkin's field and sledged down it. Coming from a town where the steepest contour is the subway pedestrian crossing we enjoyed this new exhilarating experience to the full, and were even more delighted to discover when the snowplough clattered through that it was our old friend the coalman's lorry with a clearing blade attached to its front. It was too late for Christmas shopping in town but now the road was clear we could at least go to the village. The late afternoon sky was a luminous blue, lights were appearing in the scattered farmsteads, groups of them twinkling on distant white hills like glitter on Christmas cards. It was beautiful beyond words. The village shops aglow with decorations and gifts were unfamiliar to eyes which hitherto had seen them only in the summer season, and we savoured the curious pleasure of buying Christmas cards instead of picture postcards.

Christmas passed quietly. Robert took part in the church nativity play doubling as Abraham and Joseph. Just in time we discovered that he had misinterpreted the vicar's remarkable handwriting, so that at the actual performance he intoned correctly,

'Surely God does not want me to kill my only son,'—instead of expressing a doubt about the slaughter of his old sow.

There was more snow that winter than we had experienced for years in the low lying city sixty miles to the south.

The cows, of course, were kept in their stalls all day now. They stood there chewing and I longed to take them a good book or some knitting, but they were contented enough. Except Bluebell, whose middle name must have been Houdini. She regularly unfastened her chain, lifted the lower half of the cowhouse door with her shoulder to release the latch and strolled outside to see what was happening in the hay shed. We moved the chain toggle up a few rings and got on with clearing snow from the paths to the outbuildings where, shortly afterwards, Bluebell joined us. We tied a knot in her chain to make it tighter still and before the winter was out she was wearing a padlock as big as a saucer as well.

The snowplough's rattle became a familiar sound and so did the scraping of shovels as snowbound motorists helped themselves from the pinkish heaps of grit and salt which beaded the verges. One morning about seven o'clock, just as we had discovered that the pipes were frozen and there was no water for tea, we were startled by a knock at the kitchen door. A harassed looking man stood on the threshold gazing in wonderment at our pale gaslight and told us that his lorry had run off the road on the hill. He supposed, he said with clearly diminishing hope, that we hadn't a phone? But we had, we told him proudly, and showed him into the pitch black back hall giving him a little kelly lamp for company.

He returned to the kitchen like a man in a dream, looking about him disbelievingly. We gave him a cup of tea, apologizing cheerfully for its queer colour. We had got the water from the cowhouse, we explained. Those bits in it were probably only rust from the tank. He seemed nervously uncomfortable and though we pressed him to stay until the snow stopped, he wouldn't. Must get back to his lorry. Somebody was coming out to help him, he said quickly, and he flashed us a forced smile of thanks as he stepped outside again.

An hour later, when we went out to see if the road was clear enough for Gordon to go to work we saw the man still waiting, stamping his feet and clapping his arms about him, but as I took a step towards him he swung round and made off into the blizzard. Funny chap, that, remarked Gordon.

Snow caused a deal of extra work with the sheep. Most of a morning which would have been better spent making Yorkshire pudding or washing nappies was taken up with trying to gather the lambs into the top field where I could be sure of them getting their share of sheep nuts. The roadmen, having their ten o'clockses in the shelter of our garage, offered to help. We began quite well by getting in all the lambs and most of the mums as well. While we were struggling to put the ewes out, the lambs hopped over the wall onto the road, Castle Farm written all over their faces. Jess turned them, sent them up through the cattle grid gate back to the moor and the whole process was begun again. At the end of an hour we had a completely empty field for the first time for months because Lambkin, in his meddling, contrary way had wandered through the blasted gates and was set fair to get himself run over on the highway.

Next morning I visited the rabble with their daily handout of hay, sheep nuts and sugar beet pulp, spreading a thick trail down the sheepwalks. While they had their heads down I grabbed the nearest lamb by the scruff of his wool — they were almost as big as the ewes, now, and weren't called lambs but hoggs, which I'd always thought were pigs — and heaved it struggling and writhing over the blasted gate. Luckily, though unusually, there were no onlookers and I contrived to net another three without witnesses to my unorthodox methods. Two more days and all the hoggs were safely contained within four field walls.

Mr Anderson was also daily feeding his sheep. He came by car, as he was lame and his home some way distant from his stray, and his flock awaited him by the ancient stone sheep beeld on the narrow road to the head of the valley. Our feeding time was earlier than theirs, which was fortunate for them but unlucky for us as they could hear our lot brawling over the sugar beet and would stampede over for an extra breakfast. Jess worked like a black to keep them at bay but as their number was four times greater than ours it was the Charge of the Light Brigade all over again. In a desperate attempt to foil them I craftily changed our feeding ground daily: down by the wall of the Browns' house one day, along a wide sheltered gully another, as close to the Scar's edge as I dared the next, leading the sheep in a different direction each time, crouching down as I ran so as not to be seen myself and begging them, in vain, to be quiet. It seldom worked. We were usually spotted and not only by the blue-bottoms either. Unfrequented as the road usually is in winter, at least three vehicles would pass as I loped along like Davy Crockett, bending double from the waist and making extravagant gestures meant to induce silence among the flock. The startled occupants would stare nervously or suspiciously according to temperament so that I should have to straighten and grin in what I hoped was a reassuring manner before going down under Mr Anderson's stampeding horde. Between its piston-like legs I would catch glimpses of the cars moving slowly on, round-eyed faces peering incredulously until hidden by the bend in the road.

It wasn't only at feeding time, either, that I was forced to play Indian Scouts. Simple trips to the village for a tin of Elastoplast tended to take on proportions of a rag week procession. Unfairly, for the first quarter of a mile, the bank slopes so steeply that I had to push my bike at cripple's pace to its highest point where the head-of-the-valley road leads off. Thus handicapped I was a magnet for knots of hopeful sheep and long before I had reached the top I had attracted all our flock and most of Mr Anderson's; they streamed out behind like the wake of a ship as I pedalled downhill at breakneck speed, eventually leaving them to wash up around the church like breakers on the shore. Of course I picked them up again on the return journey but this was not so embarrassing as playing the Pied Piper in the village.

10 Measles would be Nice

Spring came at last, scintillating as champagne. The curlews' kettle started boiling again, the cuckoo took over the summer shift from Derek, bluetits recommenced their mouselike scratching and squeaking behind the living room window frame, and wooden birdhouses fashioned by Robert sprouted from trees and outbuildings in such great numbers that we feared an increase in the rates.

Larches in farmyard and forest quickly intensified to a colour so remarkable that I couldn't find words to describe it until one day I had an idea and looked out some paint colour charts. I thumbed through a dozen or more gradations of green until I found the nearest corresponding shade. *Larch green*, it said on the reverse, and when you think about it that is the only accurate adjective.

The plum suckers donned frilly white petticoats, recalling their snow laden winter appearance. Snowdrops retired in favour of wood anemones, violets and primroses. The garden cleared of its weeds gleamed with more than a dozen varieties of daffodil.

Jess, now five years old and the mother of a single puppy suddenly went mad with spring fever and increased her family by six. But most exciting of all to us, up on the moor little white blobs started appearing alongside the dingy grey of the ewes.

Thankfully I had ceased the twice daily grub-running to the moor. (The teatime ration had been introduced to foil the rival gang, who at that time were mostly absent on unspecified business.) One good thing had come out of the exercise: I was two stones lighter. I recommend buying a flock of sheep to any would-be fashion model who can't say no to her nosh. You could almost see the pounds evaporating as, burdened with the food sacks, I staggered uphill. Binnie got quite concerned about me as I passed her house, dwindling before her very eyes. She said it was such a relief when I stopped because it was getting to look like the sack was moving under its own steam which was unsettling for the more sensitive of her visitors. So I met spring at a mere eight stone and with a couple of notches taken up in my Charley Turner.

Now, with the imminence of an increase in the flock I started going up to do the rounds eagerly, checking on every little white mushroom to see if it was ours, but it never was. I began to wonder if any of our ewes were in lamb at all and brooded long on the frailty of our au'd tup. I spent the days alternately despairing of ever having any lambs, and worrying about what we should do if we did; one day pessimistically scrutinizing wool-disguised contours and the next praying that there would be no complications and feeling like an expectant father. I had been an expectant mother on other occasions but this was quite different and worse.

Then, at last, in late April on a blue and gold evening throbbing with skylarks our first lamb arrived. Just beyond the cattle grid, he was. Knock-kneed and black-stockinged he stood shyly beside his mum. I wanted to shout the news from the housetops but Binnie and her daughter Judith had seen us and were hurrying as fast as anyone can up a one-in-four, eager to join in the adulation. Townsfolk like ourselves, they were thrilled to bits and we all fussed over that babe like nobody's business. It was at this happy moment Gordon returned from work and the way we congratulated each other you would have thought we had done it all ourselves, until Gordon said that he thought the ewe was Lambkin's mother and as she hadn't been able to feed him she probably wouldn't feed this one, either. This typical situation brought us down to earth.

We put mother and son to the lush grass of the Scar field and watched a while. The ewe couldn't believe her good luck with all that lovely grub. She immediately set to work on it, unconcernedly walking clean over the lamb as it ducked its head under her woolly skirt. Forlornly the lamb hesitated a second then, with the optimism of youth, tried again. Irritably the ewe twitched away and glared at us, jaws working fifteen to the dozen. Couldn't be bothered, she said shortly. Take him away and give him a bottle.

Unceremoniously Gordon upskelled her and squeezed her teats. She had milk, all right: it spurted right up his shirt sleeve. I put the quivering baby to a teat and the soft mobile lips sucked blissfully. At the opposite end a clean white tail vibrated like catkins in the wind. After a few minutes Gordon let the ewe right herself and we all watched anxiously to see if she would accept the lamb. She returned to her feeding as if she hadn't eaten for a week but at least she didn't spurn her offspring. Too late, she said huffily. Her figure was spoiled now anyway.

From then on new lambs appeared daily and were taken into the field where there was good grazing for their mothers. Then one day Robert found Twiggy, an inanimate scrap lying in the heather.

As it was obviously dead I moved on to take care of the living, leaving Robert contemplating his find and when he called out, rather uncertainly, that he had seen it move I merely attributed it to wishful thinking, but to please him I went back and picked it up. It was the tiniest thing you ever saw. Obviously premature, it was no fatter than my two hands pressed flat together but wet and cold though it was, it really did hold a flutter of life.

I snuggled the sticky creature inside my jacket and we hurried home to dry it in the warm kitchen. Cleaned of the yellowish slime we could see that though perfectly formed in miniature, her hooves were grey, soft and rubbery, and instead of wool, she wore shiny, silvery-white silk. She was unable to lift her head—too weak even to suck, so milk and glucose was squeezed into her tiny mouth from a plastic bottle, drop by drop, about an eggcupful every two hours. There was no lack of helpers—in daylight, anyway. Mother, the boys, Binnie, Judith and Barbara Bruce, a paying guest making her second visit, all craved the favour but handsomely allowed me to have a go in the night.

Twiggy's bed was a cardboard carton lined with old nappies from which she was lifted for each feed, but after the second day when she had seemed too feeble to survive, she suddenly began to gain strength until, on the morning of the fourth day, I found her out of the box and lying close to the back door for coolness.

Now she refused to stay in the box at all so was upgraded to the major league in a pen close by the cowhouse. There she had plenty of company as it was the home of seven other bottle babies. Three of them had been given to us by another farmer who hadn't the time to cope with them, but the others were our own, rescued one by one from predicaments rivalling the Perils of Pauline: trapped between rocks in the beck, hanging over a branch high up in the Scar, taken from a milkless mother or just found wandering with no visible means of support. Before long we had twelve bottle fed lambs on the books. We fed them three at a time, a bottle in each hand and one gripped between the knees, and by the time one feed was over and the bottles scalded it was time for the next. Sometimes mother helped with daytime feeds and Gordon, if he was home in time, with the evening one.

The last was usually very late and carried out by lamplight. The light always disturbed the calves in a nearby pen who bellowed loudly about discrimination, wondering where their supper was and, to add emphasis to their remarks, kicked the wooden partition with a noise like thunderclaps. Next door Jess howled like a prophet of doom. She felt obliged to do that whenever the calves shouted. It strangled her all up inside otherwise and was much better out. The puppies screamed hysterically. Got a good voice, hadn't she, their mum, they yapped admiringly.

Weak with laughter, Gordon and I sat in the straw of the lamb pen, leaning helplessly against the wall, clutching slobbery bottles which threatened to disappear down hungry gullets. The lambs which weren't making sucking noises like bathwater running out were yelling impatiently for their turn, untying our shoe laces and stamping us into the ground. Outside, Jess and her pack in full cry like a hungry night in Siberia competed with trumpeting elephants madly crashing a road through the jungle. Nothing like it was ever heard in Bellfield Avenue. What with one thing or another we were not sorry when the lambs were old enough to be penned outside in a sheep-netting enclosure which Gordon made for them at the far side of the house and out of earshot of the farmyard.

All the entries in my diary at that time end with either 'very tired' or 'very, very tired'. The good weather had broken and lambs were being born into a very wet world indeed. The sound of water was everywhere, percolating through the heather and making streams of dry gullys where sheep were wont to shelter, feeding the beck which turned brown with peat and roared like fire drawn up a chimney. The ground was a sponge which sucked at my boots, and my clothing was so continuously damp that I thought I might sprout like peas on blotting paper. Mist shrouded the sheepwalks and many a motionless ewe proved, on investigation, to be only another crouching boulder. Up there it was bleak to the point of torture and to come down to our sheltered valley and the welcoming warmth of the kitchen was a taste of heaven. The Rayburn's glow was a magnet to the tradesmen, too.

'Bitter cold on top, Mrs Fussey,' they said. 'It's a different world down here.'

Then it started to snow again and Gordon caught flu.

One night we were awakened by a bullfight in the calf field. At any rate we couldn't think of anything else that would account for the blares and bellows that threatened to loosen the window frame.

Complacently exempt because of his flu, Gordon pulled the blankets closer and said, didn't I think I ought to go and find out what was the batter? No, I replied firmly, and tried to blot out the row with the eiderdown. A fat chance I had, what with Gordon monopolizing the bedding as if by divine right, and a foghorn contest blasting into the window, so I grudgingly tore myself from my warm nest and felt for my clothes. I knew I had got my trousers on back to front as soon as I started descending the stairs, and as I groped through dining room and pantry I thought nostalgically of electric lights, remembering belatedly that there was a torch upstairs by the bedside for such contingencies as this. Having by this time arrived at the warm kitchen I rebelled at the idea of going back. Besides, outside the platinum moon shone on the snow and illuminated the kitchen well enough to enable me to light the gas lamp—if my sleep-clumsy fingers hadn't swept the box of matches off the mantelpiece. The floor was in deep shadow but I was darned if I was going to go back through that ice house of a pantry for the torch so I crawled about on hands and knees playing blind man's buff with wellingtons and table legs until a particularly exasperated swipe sent the coke hod rocking; as I clasped it to my bosom, the matchbox fell out along with about a pound of potato peelings and some pieces of coke which I knelt on. Engrossed with my thoughts I lit the lamp and pulled on wellington boots which were full of tea leaves again. People misjudged when emptying the tea-strainer into what they thought was the coke hod. It happened all the time.

I plodded through the snow feeling distinctly uncomfortable. It wasn't the tea leaves and potato peelings or even my trousers which, to be sure, were having a peculiar effect on my gait, but a hard lump in my sock told me that a suspender had become unhooked and had slipped down my leg. This was before the age of tights and the suspenders were detachable ones.

My imagination projected beasts rampaging all over the vegetable garden but as I rounded the end of the house I came across a scene of idyllic tranquillity. The moon riding high in a milky sky stippled the crisp white ground with glitter and plated the holly hedge with silver. The hedge framed a pretty picture. Deliberately posed against the contrasting white background of the field three black Angus stirks stood modestly batting their eyelashes at me. They were all wearing their digger hats, I noticed — one ear pricked, the other down — and Iris looked particularly fetching. The hair on her forehead grew in a twirl which cried out for a diamanté clip, and tonight she had one, a glittering brooch of snowflakes.

Nobody spoke and we looked at each other in silence. I remembered Topsy as we had first seen her. A 'bad doer', she was bony and listless with no appetite for food, caring little for rearing-nuts and flatly refusing even to look at milk . . . until the day Gordon gave her a bucket of detergent by mistake. As the milk supply diminished the older animals were given proportionately more water with it, and coming in one day and seeing the pail of cloudy liquid standing on the kitchen floor, Gordon, thinking he would save me a journey, poured it into the stirks' trough.

'But that was washing-up liquid,' I gasped, when he returned the empty bucket.

Without a word we shot round to the calf field. Topsy was just sucking up the last drops, blissfully smacking her lips and looking hopefully for more.

She didn't die: in fact she never looked back after that and I have recommended the treatment to every vet I have met since. (Our vet has had a succession of assistants; they don't seem to stay long after they have been to Westwath.)

The third of the trio was Bully-Beef, named by presentiment rather than sentiment. He looked like Joe Louis and expected, and got, a warm drink every night.

No-one seemed prepared to offer any explanation for the hullabaloo, and with the cold from the tea leaves numbing my toes, I made a few remarks and hobbled back to the warmth of the kitchen. There I kicked off my boots any old how, turned off the light and limped back to bed.

I'll swear that they deliberately timed it so that the next outcry shattered the night just as well-earned sleep enveloped me. Galvanized we leaped upright.

'Wha's that?' said Gordon wildly, then groaned, 'Oh, it's theb. Thought you were going to see to theb.'

'I *did*,' I insisted. 'There's nothing the matter with them. They can go into their hut and go to sleep, like me.' And I pressed a finger firmly to each ear and lay in rigid determination while Gordon tossed and groaned beside me. Still the roaring went on, gaining volume if anything.

'They're hungry,' Gordon muttered.

'What!'

'Hungry. It's the cold. Take 'b some hay.'

'But it's the middle of the night and I've just –' I gave up. Gordon was snoring again, anyway. I fell out of bed. Dazedly I searched for boots in the farthest corners of the kitchen. In a dream I trudged down to the barn and collected a bundle of hay. Sleepwalking I retraced my steps up the path, round the corner past the house to the calf field. I heaved the hay over the gate to land at the feet of the gratified trio who, once more, stood silent and sedate, and shivered convulsively. I foresaw that I should be the next to be bed-bound with flu and brightened considerably at the thought.

Back upstairs Gordon was sitting bolt upright in bed. He had a haunted look.

'Beed havig a nightmare,' he said. 'Thought subbody smashing glass, lamps and thigs, all over.' He flopped back on the pillow and sighed despairingly. 'I'll never sleep now.'

I felt completely cheered. Life had its compensations.

11   Poetry, Pets and Plumbing

'Gans doon, dis she?' said Will Arrowsmith attentively, thrusting his thumbs in his braces and leaning comfortably against
his milkstand. 'Aye, some on 'em are guilty on it.'

Will was our neighbour and tenant of Castle Farm, the
lodestone of our footloose sheep. Not a big man, nevertheless
he was great in heart and commonsense, as friendly and alert
as a robin and sent by our guardian angel to keep an eye on us.
Not that he watched us or interfered with our weird doings in
any way but whenever we needed advice or physical aid he was
always ready to lend a hand or an ear. He was like that with
everyone. One Sunday morning Gordon went up there in quest
of a calf dose and found most of the neighbourhood on a
similar mission — if it wasn't medicine it was sheep dip, rat
poison or just good counsel. Nothing seemed to be too much
trouble.

It was information I was after this time.

'I've had one doon today, mesen,' Will went on. 'Milk fever,
tha' means.'

'Do I?' I said blankly. 'What's that?'

Milk fever, Will explained, is a misfortune which often over-
takes cows after calving: the good milkers, usually. They fall
into a coma which used to be fatal until it was discovered that
the calcium deficiency which caused it could be corrected by
injecting liquid calcium into the animal. If she did gan doon,
said Will, I had to send for him. The last sentence was the only
one I cared for the sound of at all.

We had been country dwellers for just over a year and
spring had really got into its stride. Creamy bird-cherry
foamed out of every wood and hedgerow and the horse chest-

nuts were thick with coconut pyramids piled on green glaze-ware plates. The marshy ground surrounding the hummock in the Holme field had been the route of a royal progress by King Midas. It was manifest in the solid band of gold where the perfect chalices of marsh marigolds gleamed and shimmered in the sunshine. It was there that, early one morning, Rosie's calf was born. We first saw him, a sturdy little black bull, standing up to his knees in the bright flowers. And if that hadn't been contrived for our benefit I'll eat my hat.

There had been no difficulty about that birth and, apart from Rosie's refusing to recognize him as her child — couldn't think where he'd come from; *she* hadn't done anything — and, in consequence my having to milk an udder like an over-inflated football with blisters, and Rhoda, who was mater-nally-minded being so overcome with excitement that she gave no milk at all that day . . . apart from that everything was plain sailing.

But now Bluebell's production date was only a few weeks distant and this we were anticipating with misgivings. She always went, said old Rust cryptically, pursing his lips and looking grave, down. His voice was sepulchral to a degree.

'Down where?' of course we asked, wondering whether to expect her to descend like Euridice into the underworld, or sink like a deep sea diver amid an uprush of bubbles.

Mr Rust looked at us as if we weren't right in the head, and said that that was why Bluebell's chain in the cowshed was fastened to the bar with binder twine. So he could cut it when she went down. We had always thought it was tied up like that to mend it, like everything else was, and we still didn't know why she went down or what it was like when she did it because Mr Rust, feeling that he had already been too generous with information, evaded telling us anything further. So I went up the road to see Will.

Evening milking was just over as I approached Castle Farm and Will's lovely herd of Friesians was swaying out of the farmyard and crossing the road to the pasture. The children, Will and Joan's four and our own Robert and Antony, were standing about, watching for traffic, and Pauline grinned at me, calling out something I didn't quite catch about a whistle and running — just a casual remark, I thought. Lost in admiration of the animals, and thanking my lucky stars I hadn't that lot to milk by hand, I only vaguely heard the high, shrill note that came from the direction of the farmyard, but the next second I was standing alone in the middle of the road without a cow or a child in sight. But not for long. As I cast a bewildered glance around, I saw lumbering towards me from the yard gateway, large as life and more than twice as natural, Billy the Bull. I don't remember touching the garden gate but there I was at the other side of it and behind the garden wall in a rather crowded corner with six children.

Will gave me a lot of advice which would have been very good for me if I could have understood what he said. Will and I are both Yorkshire born and bred, and I pronounce putty just as he does (unfortunates from lesser counties, knowing no better, would spell it pootty) but whereas I fondly believe my accent would be readily understood in Bury St Edmunds and Basingstoke, Will's would be more at home over the sea in Scandinavia. Not only are many North Riding words Old Norse but with true Yorkshire thrift the countryman makes full use of every single letter so whereas a wasteful southerner would squander the second vowel in words like beast and head the North Yorkshireman gets his full money's worth favouring equally both halves of the words: *Bee-ast,* he says, and *hee-ad.* But that's all right with me. So long as I can understand sentences like, 'I'll come if you're stuck,' or 'Dean't be afeared to send for me', I can get by very nicely.

At least we now knew what to expect, which was something, so we relegated the problem of Bluebell's theatrical calving into the background while, taking advantage of the longer evenings, we crammed in more and more work. There had been no opportunity to dig over the vegetable garden during the winter and I started a belated campaign against the ever present couch grass. At the same time there was Antony's eighth birthday party to prepare, the farm accounts to do, the bungalow to make ready for the new season's tenants, the house, ditto for visiting friends and, just to make certain that Satan wouldn't find our hands idle, we had another water crisis.

With the first item one of the roadmen came to our aid again. He owned a small cultivator.

'I 'ave this ploo-like,' is what he actually said, and hand-somely offered to ploo us over, repeating the expression so often that we began to think of the machine quite affection-ately as the ploo-like and greeted it as an old friend when in due course it was delivered. It was parked in the farmyard awaiting the evening and the operator, and Bluebell, coming across it suddenly as she rounded the corner, nearly had her calf on the spot.

The cows were like that. Anything, we had discovered, at all out of the ordinary or not in its usual place was liable to bring on an attack of the vapours or, at the very least, a horrified examination carried out at full neck-stretch. Gordon's coat, for instance, draped over the step ladder under the old Keswick apple tree behind the cowshed set Rhoda quivering all over, eyes popping like chapel hatpegs, and Rosie stood lost in thought for all of five minutes before an enamel bowl balanced on top of a blue plastic bag of builders' sand leaning against the calfpen.

Antony's party took days to prepare. It was not the baking, which was labour enough, goodness knows, but I had ambi-tiously decided to set a treasure hunt, twelve and a half acres in which to lay the scent being an opportunity too good to miss. It was also a big area to quarter seeking out suitable hiding places for clues, and the clues themselves had to be made to rhyme to be seemly.

The first one, I felt, was amateurish, 'Behind the duckhouse in the yard. Find the next clue. It isn't hard,' but by the time I had penned, 'Cross the wath and seek a tin. Find another clue therein,' I was getting into my stride and the last, 'You've almost won so off you run to where time's measured by the sun', (the old sundial, of course) was worthy, I felt, of the Bard himself.

Two sets of clues for two teams travelling in opposite direc-tions severely taxed my inventive powers and the composing of them took the best part of a week. It took the children perhaps a quarter of an hour to complete the course, and on the following afternoon some of them returned and begged me to do them another one then and there and it didn't matter about the prizes.

So there I was feeling like Milton's poet soaring in the high

69

regions of his fancies and wondering what could possibly rhyme with cowhouse, while I scrubbed out the bungalow, washed curtains and untangled Twiggy from the sheepnetting fence.

This business of untangling Twiggy was beginning to take precedence over everything else. You would have thought that a quarter of an acre of grassy pasture equipped with all mod cons comprising a lean-to daytime shelter and a dry cosy shed for nights would have spelt luxury for five small lambs. (The others had died despite Gordon's tireless ministrations. Every night after work, sometimes until long past midnight, he had devotedly but unavailingly doctored them.) It did for four of them but Twiggy complained unceasingly that she was imprisoned in a little cage and we needn't think she didn't know about the RSPCA. If she wasn't eating she was bawling and I was wearing a groove round to their pen until I tumbled to it that she did it because she enjoyed the excitement of seeing me tear up in a cloud of dust and not because the others were bullying little her as she would have me believe.

It took about a day for her to think up something else. It was a continuous pitiful bleat which caught my attention, a cry completely lacking the familiar belligerence, utterly convincing and guaranteed to fetch me at the double. There she stood, a picture of pathos, head through a hole in the sheepnetting, anchored by her minute horns. Chained up just like a little slave girl, she wailed, for ages and hadn't I heard her shouting?

Delighted with the success of that little scheme she worked it threadbare. Half a dozen times a day I answered the pathetic cry to find our little Pearl White pilloried in the netting, and after a week of it there was nothing I would have liked better than to throw rotten tomatoes at her. Things came to a head the day before the first bungalow people were due to arrive. It was a quarter to five in the morning when I disentangled Twiggy for the first time that day and midday, the seventh. I was desperately washing windows and hanging curtains when for the eighth time her cry throbbed across the garden and I shut off all sympathy, turned a deaf ear and let her get on with it until, having to stop for tea anyway, I stormed round to find that she had knitted herself in and out of so many holes that she looked like a string bag. And a fine time I had getting her out of that.

That pen was big enough for five *cows*, said Gordon crossly as he bored postholes in the stony ground and stretched more netting between. The new pen was big enough for half a dozen elephants, enclosing green, lush grass simply oozing goodness, and Twiggy, without giving it a second glance marched determinedly over to the new fence, thrust her head through to the stony path beyond and petulantly chewed up a withered brown leaf.

However, the new enclosure was a great success. It gave the lambs a new interest and me a breather, for now it contained the end of the holly hedge. There is a story that Peter the Great got a terrific kick out of being pushed in a wheelbarrow through John Evelyn's famous holly hedge at Saye's Court. It must have been an interesting sight but for sheer spectacle our lot had him beaten into a cocked hat. Shooting through it like javelins they played last one's a cissy back and forth, emerging each time covered with bliss and prickles. It wasn't half fun. Like being in a circus.

They ought to have been in a circus. In fact sometimes I thought they were. In the mornings, for instance, when with breakfast bottles at the ready I approached their hut. At the sound of my voice a drumming would start, sporadic at first as they scrambled to their feet and gathered their wits, but gaining in volume and speed until it sounded as if, driven by centrifugal force, they were galloping round and round half way up the walls like the Wall of Death. They whizzed round like that until their momentum ejected them like tracer bullets through the open door. Small visitors, importantly accompanying me to help carry the bottles, were shaken rigid and lost faith in Mary's little lamb on the spot.

Anyway these divertissements kept our minds off Bluebell's approaching confinement and threatened foundering as also did the eccentricities of our water supply.

For some time we had noticed the cistern filling or a tap turned on in the yard tended to reduce the degree of success with which we rinsed our teeth and more than one person, modestly clutching a bath towel, had had occasion to lean out of the bathroom window and roar for someone to turn that so and so hose pipe off. From this we deduced that the tank above the wood was due for its annual scrub out. For numerous reasons (see all previous paragraphs) we had not got round to doing this and consequently on the very day that the Cawkwells and Evans's were coming to stay in the bungalow everything dried up simultaneously; a trickle of something like red rust was the best any tap could offer.

I went weak-kneed with horror and rehearsed a hundred times what I would say to the new arrivals. There had been occasions during the previous year when I had had to explain to incoming tenants that the drinking water was that funny brown colour because the heavy rain we were having was stirring up the peat; there were times when I bathed in water so peat-enriched that I felt like Tollund Man; but I could hardly tell them that there wasn't a drop of any colour and would they care to share our damp face flannel. After all, there are limits.

Once more the neighbours came thundering to the rescue — Binnie, this time. Filling two milkchurns, which normally stood in their doorway for the accommodation of walking sticks, with water from their own spring, she and her son Richard brought them down in the boot of their car and delivered them onto our doorstep. This was more of a sacrifice than it seems because that spring also had its little ways. Leaving mother to dole out the rations, which she did as jealously as if we were a bunch of legionnaires lost in the desert, Gordon and I went up to the top tank.

I had not been before and was fascinated by the equipment Gordon deemed necessary to take with us. Scrubbing brushes, of course, buckets, a sack or two, a short length of guttering, an eight foot ladder, a couple of jemmies. *Jemmies!* Whatever were we going to do, for goodness sake? I hoped it was legal. We loaded all the stuff into the car and went round by road, a distance of about one and a half miles, to Ellers Farm where we left the car in a flock of geese and lugged our unlikely impedimenta across a field. We were now just outside the top fence of the forest and immediately above tree-hidden West-wath which, despite the distance by road, was only a couple of hundred yards below.

Set in the grass were three enormous slabs of concrete forming a square. So this was our famous top tank. I found out what the jemmies were for when my husband (the same who had promised to cherish me only a dozen years before) pressed one tenderly into my hand and suggested that I prised up one of the slabs. True he was levering away at the other end and it was with no more trouble than it would take to brush aside the Pyramid of Cheops that we shoved it along until a gap two feet wide appeared across the middle. What I could see down there in the darkness looked very wet indeed and utterly resistible and I watched without envy as Gordon slotted in the ladder and descended the first few rungs.

Now I could see that water was running into the tank through an inlet pipe a few inches from the top on the field side. Gordon explained that this was coming from the spring some distance away. Choosing his phrases carefully and using words of one syllable so that I could follow, he went on to tell me that there was an outlet pipe near the bottom of the tank on the forest side which carried the supply down to Westwath. When the tank was full, the surplus water ran through another outlet pipe at the top and formed a little stream, the very one which tinkled out of the wood and separated our Holme and back fields on its way to the beck. Actually, I had already noticed the outflow because the first thing I had done on arrival was to slip in the mud surrounding it and fill my boot.

The first step was to stop the inflow. This Gordon did by wedging the length of guttering under the duct so that the stream was channelled straight out of the overflow, which was what the poor thing had wanted to do all along; while Gordon was attending to these technical matters I stood and admired the view. It was like one of those fascinating picture maps.

Far over the green bowl in which lay Westwath the moors rolled to the horizon. At this time of the year broad sweeps of young green bracken mingled with blotches of pink where the cross-leaved heath bloomed. Later as the ling bells opened in their millions, the moors would be a wash of pinky purple. The Browns' sun-soaked house stood out clearly against this background. I could even see Binnie in bright red trousers labouring over a flower bed. Above the house the ancient sheep beeld, sprawling like a starfish on the hillside, seemed about to slide down the chimney, and way below a glimpse of

our own pantiled roof, all but submerged in breakers of green-
ery. On the other side of the narrow road which vanished over
the heat-hazy skyline on its way to the hidden village, and from
this viewpoint looking dangerously close to it, the deep gorge
of the Scar dropped away abruptly and dramatically, the
wavering wall of our almost-ready-for-mowing top fields seemingly teetering on the very edge.

While I was refreshing my soul with beauty Gordon had
been doing things with buckets and I was just about to give
him my reluctant attention and insincere offer of help when
my eyes did a rapid double take to the top fields. What, for
heaven's sake, was the matter with the grass! For the past few
weeks the fields had been semi-successfully barred to sheep to
give the grass chance to grow for hay. To help it along the
grass had been treated with chemical fertilizer, or manishment
as we call it up here, goodness knows why. It comes in big
plastic bags, looks like pelleted seed and is scattered by means
of a mechanical spreader drawn behind a tractor. At least that
is how it is done on conventional well regulated farms such as
Will Arrowsmith's.

From our top fields bright blue or red manishment
spreaders could be seen puffing out clouds of pellets as they
crept round and round the high fields of Castle and Ellers,
Rowan Head and Ghyll House farms which ringed our valley,
and a proper Charlie I felt hiking up and down ours chucking
the stuff out of a plastic bucket by means of a hearth shovel.
Adjured by my boss to spread it evenly, I had fixed my sights
on a landmark at the farther side and walked towards it flinging shovelsful of fertilizer in wide arcs which showered about
my ears like hailstones and got into my hair. Back and forth I
went, refilling the bucket after each crossing, starting farther
up the hill each time. To relieve the monotony I tried tossing it
upwards, immediately following through with an overarm
swipe with the shovel, but this was even worse for the hair and
earned derisive comment from the roadmen. In all, I had
lugged half a ton of fertilizer, scattering it meticulously to
ensure the best possible benefit to every infant blade, and from
this vantage point at Ellers Farm the natural outcome was to
all eyes revealed.

It looked like sky writing in reverse. Where the fertilizer had fallen the grass grew strongly in marked contrast to the rest. Loops, scrolls and curlicues tapered across the meadow; flourishes and furbelows dashed off with artistry decorated the borders, and a series of arabesques in the topmost corner proclaimed a master hand. I was absolutely rivetted.

By this time Gordon's bucketwork had created a morass around my feet. It would be better, he said, if I would stop staring into the blue like Cortez on Darien and empty the water into the stream.

Hurriedly, I pulled myself together and eagerly accepted the next brimming bucket — anything was better than that he come to the surface and see what I could see — feverishly throwing water in the general direction of the stream, returning the empty pails and exchanging them for full ones until at length the tank was empty.

It wasn't so bad as he had expected, said Gordon cheerfully. He'd just scrub it out and then we could go home. I was relieved to see that there was only one scrubbing brush as I didn't much fancy descending into the bowels of the earth, for from the tank emanated a chill dungeon smell.

It was pretty cold up on top now. The sun had disappeared behind misty cloud and this, combined with the sudden inactivity, set me wishing I had brought a cardigan. It was also rather boring. The mist mercifully veiled our top fields but it also obliterated the rest of the view. I would have cleared off home if I hadn't felt that my place was beside my husband, rallying him on, and besides it was a long way to walk by road. So I stood on the brink and conversed with him about my cold feet until elbowed out by two dozen enormous Friesian cows, many of them in an advanced state of pregnancy, all critically peering into the tank and considerably blocking the light.

Gordon climbed out of the tank, pulled up the ladder, removed the guttering to set the tank filling again and shuffled the concrete slabs back in place. We gathered up all the equipment, pushed our way through the crowd, crammed everything into the car and drove home, confident that all would now be well.

There was still no water issuing from the taps, though until the water level was high enough in the tank we didn't expect there would be, but when we had milked and eaten and the taps were still as dry as the Sahara it would have been plain to a one-eyed fruit bat that we were in for one of our better crises.

12   It Keeps us Occupied

It was late in the evening when we returned to the top tank and it was one o'clock in the morning when we garaged the car and sleepwalked back across the silent field, empty handed this time. We had left the housebreaking apparatus behind the forestry fence, out of the way of Charlie's cows. We were sick of the sight of the tank. We were tired, dirty, very, very wet and not the slightest bit nearer to solving the water problem. We did know what wasn't causing the bother and that was the tank. Somewhere — and our hearts plummeted like stones at the thought — between it and the farm, in the quarter of a mile of black alkathene pipe which lay buried in the ground under a jungle of forest undergrowth and the grazing land behind the bungalow, lurked the source of the trouble.

Next day while Gordon was at work I dug futile little holes all over the back field with the same unfounded faith with which I strew crosses on Find the Ball competitions. I never find the ball and I didn't locate the pipe. That evening, with inspiration that to me spelt ESP or pure fluke, (but which he pompously attributed to intelligent reasoning) Gordon found it at first shot — by the gate between the back and hay fields. He uncovered it again a few yards away inside the hayfield by the edge of the forest. Why he should have correctly presumed that it crossed underneath the gateway remains a mystery to me to this day, but he is quite overbearing about it. He sawed through the pipe which gushed forth encouragingly for two seconds flat before adopting the same inertia affected by the taps and cisterns at the farm. Up in the forest, of course. It would be. In the gathering dusk even Gordon's intellectual prowess balked at reasoning where *that* was, and after unsuccessfully trying to start something moving with the car's foot-pump, and finding it was one o'clock again, we gave up for the night.

The forest belongs to the Forestry Commission and is private but we have permission to attend to our water pipe in an emergency and being of the opinion that we had one we felt no diffidence about climbing over the fence the following evening. It is quite a young forest of mixed conifers interplanted with groups of birch and beech further leavened with other deciduous trees so it will never attain the dark, forbidding perpendicularity of most plantations but rather the romanticism of Badger's Wild Wood — threatening to Mole, perhaps, but exciting to me.

The excitement began straight away when I ripped my trousers on the single-strand barbed wire topping the stout netting fence, and continued as we tore through the arching briars and wild raspberry. Hitherto somnolent midges rose ecstatically from the chest-high bracken and welcomed us with open jaws. We wore them like halos for the rest of the night.

Up at the tank the procedure was as before except that this time I hoisted up the slopping buckets — eighty-nine of them — while Gordon went down to the field to disconnect the pipe where he had severed it the previous evening.

Shades of Bulldog Drummond, Richard Chandos, Dick Barton; I could almost hear the Devil's Gallop as I descended deeper into the tank following the lowering water level. Trickles plinked and plonked from the ill-fitting joint between the guttering and the inlet pipe, and moisture oozed down the walls. It was dark in there too, cold, probably, though I didn't notice that, I was sweating so much in my eagerness to empty the thing and get out of it before Petersen or Moriarty, with fiendish laugh, levered the concrete slab shut. A figure loomed overhead and a beam of light gleamed on the murky water. I swallowed a shriek and was at the top of the ladder without touching all the rungs.

Wasn't it empty yet, Gordon enquired with surprise. Oh, well, never mind, he went on with the air of one who has to do everything. He'd finish it. He'd located the stop tap at the top of the forest and disconnected that, too, which should help.

When the tank was empty he set to work with the foot pump

and despatched me down the forest to see what was happening at the other end; when I reported that nothing whatever was, and what's more I had torn my trousers again he decided to let the tank fill up to the outlet hole and try to push the water through. Leaving him standing on the pump with both feet, back braced against the concrete top and working himself into a lather, I blundered down the now familiar path to examine the cut pipe once more. This time it was exuding a trickle of what looked like Worcester Sauce.

Peat, said Gordon when I told him. Blast, there was nothing else for it but to cut the pipe in sections and push a heavy wire down it, which we couldn't do that night because we hadn't any . . . besides it was already past midnight again. Gordon tore his trousers when climbing over the fence.

Next day I phoned the agricultural suppliers and ordered a prodigious amount of heavy gauge single-strand fencing wire, which they interpreted as barbed wire and duly delivered. Mr Rust appeared after an absence of some days and told me that alkathene piping shouldn't corrode. I explained that it hadn't, that it was silted up with fine peat and we were going to clean it out.

Mr Rust frowned darkly and repeated that it couldn't corrode and it had never happened before. I repeated that it was silt and would he mind giving me some idea of the route the pipe took through the forest? (We had a rough idea now, but half way up was a bit of an escarpment which confused us rather.)

He glowered under drawn eyebrows while he thought how not to tell me then, rather lamely, fell back on his catch phrase that alkathene couldn't corrode and added that there was no need for all this bother and had we tried turning the yard tap on?

Patiently I described the silt: black and very fine, the texture of face powder, and it was blocking the pipe and we should have to clear it out and if he would just indicate where it was laid it would be a great help.

Fiercely he stared at the ground, then flinging out an arm in a wide irritable gesture which embraced two fields, acres of forest and about twenty-five square miles of moor he said,

'It goes up there!' While I stood grinding my teeth he went

on grudgingly that he was going round to Ellers Farm anyway, so he would mark where it started to go down. Not that there was any need for it, as in his opinion it was only an airlock; later that evening when we went up to make a start we found that he had placed an earthen drain pipe about ten yards below the stop-tap in the one place we were reasonably sure about anyway.

It was a fortnight of weekends and late nights before the sweet sound of filling cisterns gladdened our hearts. Toilets flushed and filled instantly, musically, luxuriously. Taps gushed forth with a pressure we had not known all the time we had lived at Westwath. No longer did the use of the yard tap — the lowest point of the system — prevent the operation of the others. We could clean our teeth without inconvenience at the same time as the bungalow people drew water for washing up. Dear Carmichaels. They had succeeded the equally tolerant Cawthorns and Evans's and despite their numerous visitors had coped with the water shortage like Trojans. Country folk themselves, they took it all in their stride and sent us Christmas cards for years afterwards.

Gordon had traced the pipe by digging long trenches at intervals across its suspected route. Then he had cut through it in fifty-foot sections and, he at Camp One, using pliers for a grip, had forced and coaxed the thick wire down to me at Camp Two, fifty feet below, where I hauled on the corkscrew end he had made, and we worked it back and forth, periodically flushing water through until the silt (which had settled inside the one-and-a-half-inch gauge pipe so thickly that the remaining hole wouldn't accept a pencil) was completely eradicated. Umpteen lengths we treated like this; it was a tiring, wet, hand-crippling, sweaty, midge-ridden occupation.

Mr Rust examined the small piece of pipe complete with stoppage which Gordon wished to preserve as a memento and talking point, and with one devastating prod of a fat finger cleared out the contents.

That's why he'd had alkathene pipe laid in the first place, he said triumphantly. So that it wouldn't corrode. And anyway, he fired his parting shot, it had never happened before.

Compared with all that the next few weeks passed tranquilly

as late June should, with hot fragrant days, and nights so short as to be hardly worth mentioning, the nightjars treadling their sewing machines fifteen to the dozen so as to be done by morning.

The five remaining ducks all went broody at once, heaped together in one small nest, heads sticking out at all angles like the arms of Shiva, and anyone who had the effrontery to peep into their hut during this critical period was greeted by vexed hissings and chunterings from five gaping bills, which dipped and swayed in unison. They looked like the Andrews Sisters. The drake, Sir Francis, fussed and fretted over them like any human expectant father. We had long marvelled at the responsibility he patently felt for his wives, in complete contrast to the cockerel who stood no nonsense from his harem. Apart from racing over to the source of each cackle to make sure the egg was one of his, he couldn't be bothered at all.

But Sir Francis devoted himself to Annabelle, Annabelle, Annabelle, Annabelle and Jemima, whistling them up at mealtimes, anxious that each should have her share. At night he would shepherd them into their hut, himself hopping inside only when all were accounted for, waddling back and forth between the main party and a straggler when going on expeditions, (the laggard was usually Jemima who was lame and therefore the only one we could identify) and now pacing up and down outside the hut to keep intruders at bay.

One day, satisfied that they had fulfilled their moral obligation as incubators and that they couldn't be blamed if nothing had come of it, the quintet with one accord left the nest, shrugging feathers into place like the Mothers' Union settling its corsets, and filed off to the beck and the good life, Sir Francis, with relief and reliability written all over him, bringing up the rear. It wasn't their fault either, as I found out when I went to clear away the wasted eggs and discovered that for nearly a fortnight the balmy ha'porths had been sitting on a solitary pot one.

The Ministry of Agriculture came for the summer inspection of the cows. Very much in awe of their representative, I chattered brightly to cover my apprehension as I led him round to the field behind the bungalow. He walked like a somnambulist saying little, remembering our individual approach to lamb rearing and obviously wondering to what eccentricities he was to be introduced now.

The motley Westwath herd of three grazed unconcernedly in the shadow of two oaks just as if the granting of Hill Cow Subsidy didn't matter a bit: brown, black, off-white, pinkish, one horned and two polled — as utterly unmatched in size and colour as it was possible to be. I stole a nervous glance at the Ministry of Agriculture who was staring at them in utter disbelief, his sheaf of board-backed papers hanging unheeded at his side. My heart dropped into my socks but before I could stammer out explanations and excuses and offer to surrender my herdsman's stripes unconditionally, he completely bowled me over by professing himself delighted with their condition, congratulating us on the way we had looked after them and pronouncing them three fine cows.

They were, too. Rhoda's red coat was as buffed and burnished as a favoured conker, Rosie's had the subtle inner glow of a polished cameo and Bluebell, well, Bluebell's coat looked like well-brushed *new* railwayman's trousers. She still hadn't calved, was now a few days overdue and had a girth like the boiler of the Royal Scot. She stood there, firmly planted among the daisies, looking like Giles's cartoon Grandma, the knot of burdock burrs ornamenting the tuft of black curls on her forehead increasing the illusion of a hat. Truth to tell she had a lot of Grandma's ornery ways, too.

During these hot, debilitating days mother, Roger and I actually managed to steal the odd hour's leisure, drinking tea in the garden with Binnie and Judith, gazing into the welcome shade of trees on our lawn, enjoying the wide panoramic view of the valley from Binnie's. Returning from Binnie's one day, we saw the dustmen emptying our bin for the first time since we started taking it across to the roadside. For months we had been carrying the full bin out early in the morning and fetching it back empty at night without ever knowing who was responsible for it. I leaned to the theory that it was fairies or hobs but unless Robin Goodfellow wears glasses and a flat cap it can't be he.

This idyllic smoothness inevitably had its gritty bits, such as the time when I was too hot to change into jeans for milking. Rhoda, disliking this sudden departure from the norm, lashed out with her hind leg and ripped my cotton skirt from waist-band to hem, and for a week I had a leg the colour of ripe plums with opal highlights. Then there was the occasion Antony came home from school, offered to empty a basket of weeds for me and threw weeds, basket and himself in his best school clothes into the deepest pool in the beck.

On Robert's birthday we sweltered under almost tropical heat: stepping outside was like walking into an oven. Inside the house the damp was almost unbelievable. Walls were soaked black up to half their height; water stood in pools on the flagged pantry floor and ran in rivulets down the painted stone fireplace surrounds, and windows and mirrors were opaque with moisture. The wallpaper in one bedroom literally fell off the walls in complete lengths and lay over the furniture like dustsheets, its wet pasty smell pervading the house. I thanked my lucky stars I had not arranged a birthday party, and with the installation of a damp-course in mind filled in the Find the Ball coupon with extra care.

That night mother discovered Robert reading under the bedclothes by the light of a birthday present torch. It was too light to use it otherwise, he complained indignantly and logically when she confiscated it.

Three days later Bluebell calved.

13   *Going, Going—Gone!*

She was near, said Old Rust portentously on Thursday afternoon, pressing pudgy hands in the hollows on either side of Bluebell's tail. Seeing that she could hardly waddle for an udder as big, round and hard as a sea-mine and furthermore was bellowing at the full extent of her lungs about her tummy-ache, that was obvious even to me — and to anyone else within a radius of five miles. I thought that Gordon would hear her at the other end of the phone when I rang the garage to tell him that everything was all right and I could cope but he wouldn't be too late, would he?

Actually, as the phone seemed to be full of frying sausages he couldn't even hear me. I screamed into the atmospherics that Bluebell was due. Going to have her calf at any time. And all he said was, What? and, Hello? and Was I still there as he couldn't quite catch what I was saying? He guessed, though, and set off home as soon as he could; it wasn't his fault that the car chose that particular evening to develop fuel pump trouble. He could keep it ticking only by jumping out and giving it a sharp tap every mile or so and jolting onto the grass verge in a vigorous conga rhythm every few hundred yards, which could have been embarrassing had a police patrol car chanced on the scene.

In the meantime, having broadcast the impending event to all the neighbourhood, Bluebell changed her tactics and stood demurely beneath the chestnut tree trying to look pale and interesting and reminding me that I knew she always went down, didn't I? Her coyness might have come over more convincingly if she could have looked less like Grandma crossed with a tough gum-chewing GI and had refrained from casting sidelong glances to see how I was taking it. As a matter of fact I was taking it very badly, counting our stock of calcium borogluconate over and over again, checking that the bran was handy for an ante natal warm mash, putting more clean sacks to warm by the Rayburn then going over the calcium again in case someone had drunk it while I wasn't looking.

Carefully not watching Bluebell I hovered about doing odd jobs: searching for eggs in the hay, emptying the muck-barrow and scrubbing it out in the beck in case it would be needed for a baby-carriage, and willing Gordon to appear until my eyes popped. When shortly before midnight he did, kicking the car as a parting shot, I felt I'd had a couple of calves myself.

Blue still stood stolidly beneath the tree, dedicatedly chewing and indicating by her determinedly turned rump that she didn't think she'd bother to calve tonight and what was the wheelbarrow parked there for? Gordon said he would wait up a while and I could go to bed and perhaps get up extra early in the morning. I woke at two thirty when Gordon came to bed. She hadn't moved, he said, and he'd had a hard day at work, a harrowing journey home expecting to be pinched for drunken driving and supposed it would be the same going back tomorrow. Today, he amended gloomily.

At three thirty I awoke again and clad in dressing gown and slippers padded past the sleeping bungalow and through the gate into the farmyard. Apart from Rosie's son Sydney stirring in the straw and an early bird warning the worms to watch out, all was silence there. I sidled between the duck and hen-houses, peered expectantly into the girls' dormitory and counted heads. There were still only three. Rosie, obviously an early riser, was tucking into her breakfast, tearing at the grass with the sound of ripping calico. Rhoda and Bluebell, resembling a pair of enormous slugs in the grey dawn light slumbered peacefully and looked as if they had every intention of having a good lie in.

I crept back to bed and overslept. At six o'clock I was back in the yard staring across the field in wonderment at the small black creature nuzzling Rhoda, who was apparently seeing to his breakfast.

At a quarter to five she'd calved, said Mr Boon in the bungalow dispiritedly, wiping bismuth from his lips. He'd hardly been asleep five minutes, what with his indigestion and that, when suddenly she'd let out this roar and frightened the daylights out of him. How I had missed it I'll never know.

Unlike human babies which are born with a built-in resistance to disease, calves receive theirs from their mother's all important first milk and the sooner they get it the better: certainly within the first six hours of their lives. And here was the baby already more than an hour old hungrily seeking nourishment from a cow almost at the end of her lactation while its own mother, bursting at the seams with colostrum enriched milk, but seemingly as devoid of maternal solicitude as her daughter Rosie, was content to hand him over to a wet nurse.

Manhandling a slippery new calf in the dew soaked grass of early morning in order to reunite him with a reluctant mother whose reverse and side step would have enchanted Victor Sylvester, while fending off an eager foster parent with determined horns, was not the ideal way to round off a very disturbed night, and we hoped we might have more success if we transferred the drama to the *mis en scène* of the cowhouse.

Needless to say, the whole thing was taking place at the end of the field farthest from the cowhouse: in the boggy patch at the bottom where it was impossible to push the wheelbarrow. So Gordon carried the calf over twenty yards of reedy marsh, turning his ankle on tussocks and losing his boots at every step, to where I waited with the sack-lined barrow. Then while I held down the kicking, squirming creature, Gordon pushed the makeshift pram, both of us hindered by the cows who were lumbering alongside like outriders in a VIP procession, every now and then making excited darts at the barrow in order to admire the new baby.

Thankfully we trundled through the gateway and made a mad dash to the cowhouse with the intention of shaking off the fans and shutting mother and son inside together, only to find that though the son part of the duo was present and correct, present also were Rhoda and Rosie, while Bluebell was back in the bog bewailing to the world that her child had been taken from her.

When at length Bluebell had been firmly fettered in her stall, the gate-crashers ejected and turned back into the field (where they leaned over the fence as near to the cowhouse as

86

possible and bawled encouragement to Bluebell and abuse at us) we found we were little better off. Bluebell wouldn't have the calf near her and her statements to this effect nearly blasted the roof off. The calf was no help at all, because not only did he have original ideas as to which end of a cow dispensed the goodies but with wildly misplaced optimism was certain that our legs would serve equally well.

Even hobbling Blue's legs and putting a teat into his mouth couldn't convince him that that was what he was searching for. Didn't fancy that rubbery thing at all, he snorted, and wished he hadn't come.

Time was getting on. Gordon was going to be late for work and the other two cows had yet to be milked so we shuffled Simon, as he came to be called, into a comfortable straw-lined pen close to his nephew, Sydney; then Gordon drew off a few pints of thick, sticky, carroty looking first milk from Bluebell into a pail and tried to coax Simon to drink from that.

Time and time again Gordon succeeded in getting the calf to suck his fingers but each time he lowered them gently into the milk Simon jerked away spluttering his distaste. Gordon's fingers were all right, he said, but that sticky stuff, ugh! Couldn't face it at this time of the morning. Reduced at last to pouring some into a bottle fitted with a black rubber lamb teat, we forced a few drops past the lollopping tongue and down the objecting throat. Making the best of that Gordon set off on his erratic way to work and I brought in the other cows and milked them.

I couldn't settle after that and spent most of the day apprehensively watching Bluebell. When I wasn't doing that I was having sessions with her son — being dragged round his pen like a sledge, hanging onto a bucket he was wearing halter fashion while the precious colostrum ran over his head like sauce on a pudding.

Sydney, next door, was horrified. All that good food going to waste. *He* had emptied his bucket, which I had given him in full view of his neighbour in the hope that it would instigate imitation, in five seconds flat. Show him again if I liked, he offered brightly.

How slowly the day passed as I prowled about watching Bluebell like a lynx. Although Rhoda and Rosie were invariably in plain view of Bluebell always managed to be out of sight. Behind the hillock in the Holme field, away over in the marsh at its end or merely blending into the shadows beneath the trees. Over and over again my heart turned a somersault as a searchlight gaze failed to find her and my life must have been shortened by about ten years as panic turned my legs to jelly.

She was always there somewhere of course. Reaching to pull down a spray of ash leaves or standing trancelike dreaming dreams and seeing visions as blamelessly as you like and I would risk leaving her for a few minutes. No sooner had I let her out of my sight than I envisaged her going down like anything and could do no other than get back on watch as fast as my legs would take me.

Occasionally I drifted across to the roadside in the hope that Will or somebody to whom I could unburden myself would pass, but not even the roadmen were about that day. The vet of all people did drive by, waving a cheerful hand in greeting. As I raised mine in reply I wildly considered stopping him and, with Ancient Mariner tenacity, detaining him until he was needed. But he was another, I remembered, who had that measuring look in his eye. Did I know, he once told me, that I was the first person ever to consult him about tapeworms in a duck? And he'd been practising for thirty years.

At five o'clock I decided on one last lap round the circuit before going indoors to prepare tea. Rhoda and Rosie, grazing by the gate, lifted enquiring heads and stared after me suspiciously, wisps of grass trailing unheeded from mouth corners. Bluebell as usual was nowhere to be seen. Not under the chestnut tree, nor in the undergrowth by the forest fence nor hidden by the fallen oak. I went round the hillock like Atlanta.

She was there all right. In the rushes at the boggy end, still and silent, a big black heap like a grounded whale. Bluebell had gone down.

On legs like overdone spaghetti I set off for Castle Farm but halfway across the wath was overtaken by Mr Boon. He had seen me on my knees by Bluebell's inert form and being familiar with her case history — it had been my only topic of conversation for days — had realized what had happened and come to offer to run me up to Castle Farm in his car.

The Arrowsmiths were just sitting down to tea when I burst in wringing my hands and uttering incoherent cries, but Will and his man, George, sized up the situation with remarkable acumen and apart from downing large cups of tea left their meal and followed forthwith. Such was our celerity and my agitation that I was quite convinced that we had done the double trip with me clinging to the running board as in the old gangster films; you could have knocked me down with a feather when I discovered that cars don't have them any more.

Bluebell still lay on her side with her head thrown back, breathing laboriously. Will produced a flutter valve — a long rubber tube with a needle affixed to one end, and without wasting any time attached one of our bottles of calcium borogluconate to the other, inserting the needle under the skin just above Bluebell's shoulder. With firm fingers he kneaded the flesh surrounding the needle, ensuring correct dispersal of the calcium which tended to build up into a swelling around the point of entry, while George held the inverted bottle high and watched the air bubbles rising. The tube was an old one and occasionally the bubbles stopped.

Memories of Dr Kildare and Emergency Ward Ten with white-coated doctors exchanging significant glances jerked across my vision like a series of film stills. I flashed a significant glance at Will who missed it because he was asking George if he'd heard about Bill To'ner's Jersey coo lowpin' t'wall and gittin' hersen kilt wi' a car (te 'ell wi' this bloody thing. He'd have ti be gettin' a new yan) and he couldn't claim off'n his insurance and to cap it all t'feller was after him fer damage to t'car.

That was when I learned that straying stock is entirely the farmer's responsibility. Even though a gate is left open by picnickers, walkers and others totally unconnected with the farm, it is the farmer who bears the cost of his own losses and that of any damage caused by the animals during the course of their peregrinations. And, I reflected gloomily, there was a right of way through the length of our calf field.

The last drop of fluid drained into the tube. A second bottle replaced the empty one and the bubbling recommenced. Bluebell was still dead to the world, her face crawling with flies despite the switch of reeds I wielded. George changed the bottle over to the other hand and rested his aching arm. I watched the bubbles rise and the watermark descend and thought about Bluebell and how fond of her we were. Will related a story about a cow of his who had been down for a week and George capped it with an anecdote about one belonging to a friend of his who hadn't got up for a month, lost all use of her legs and had to be put down. I had just resolved to sell the farm and go to sea when Blue gave a sudden heave and nearly screwed her head off backwards. This attempt to wring her own neck and be done with it was adroitly foiled by Will and the operation continued more optimistically with Bluebell showing signs of granting us the privilege of her company for some time yet.

With two pints of the hard stuff percolating through her, Blue's diehard spirit began to revive and despite the terrible blowing of her lungs she repeatedly drew up her feet in a determined effort to get out of that ignominious position; she was as mad as her hat when all she could do was wallow like a waterlogged lifeboat and get her legs tangled.

Anyway Will professed himself pleased with her, opined that she would be up within a couple of hours but if not I was to send for him again, waved aside my thanks and hurried back with George to Castle Farm and a late milking.

It was our milking time, too, so leaving a circle of children keeping watch over our heroine I went to attend to it. I had finished and was just turning Rhoda and Rosie out again when Robert cried out that Bluebell was standing up! She was up all right, but doing nothing so passive and dull as merely standing. She was yawing like a schooner in a sudden squall on an erratic course deeper into the marsh, hell-bent on impaling herself on the jagged, probing branches of the fallen oak.

In the country life is leisurely, it moves at a slower pace. Far way from the city's rat race it unbends the mind and puts things into perspective: it is a balm to the spirit. In the country there is time to stand and stare, think and dream . . . tomorrow will do, or the next day. We know this is true because visitors from town relaxing in our living room in pastel crimplene tell us so and point out how lucky we are to be living this life of eternal contentment. We, shifting uneasily from one foot to the other and hoping that that loud crashing noise outside is not the beasts breaking out again, dubiously agree and wish they would go home and let us get on with the feeding.

I thought of this again as once more I raced down the Holme field and tried to think of an equivalent situation in Bellfield Avenue. The only comparison I came up with was when Susie the goldfish died and Sammy went berserk, swimming in demented circles round his bowl for two days until I got him another mate. Harrowing though that was, it was hardly a just parallel, calling for much less exertion on my part.

With the children's help Bluebell was rounded up and, looking as if she was about to burst into 'Nellie Dean' at any moment, herded into her straw-padded stall and her shivering body covered with warm sacks. I took from her just enough milk to feed the calf so she was not robbed of the calcium and hoped she would not get mastitis through not being milked out — another of our relaxing country matters — then left her untethered for the night.

14 Summer Interlude

Bluebell felt much better next day. She must have done because while I milked the other two I could hear her behind me noisily eating her bed, but to be on the safe side Gordon drove into town to buy more calcium and to order a flutter valve, borrowing Will's in the meantime in case of emergency.

Also that day the Boons departed and the Lyttons moved into the bungalow. There were Mr and Mrs Lytton, their married daughter and her husband and their grandson, Arthur, self appointed egg-collector-in-chief. They were very nice, hailed from the Newcastle area and were utterly unintelligible. In conversation with the daughter, whose name I never learned, I could just get by, but after the first evening her husband and I communicated only with exaggerated smiles. I grinned at that man until he must have thought my mouth was locked in rigor. I just had to compensate for the fiasco when he came to speak to me as I was filling the calves' evening water buckets.

Very pleasant he was and rather shy so I was sorry when he addressed me in faultless double-dutch, for it aroused in me complete blankness. Although he repeated the whole thing twice more — I knew it was repetition because I distinctly caught the sounds 'trutt' and 'fush' in roughly the same places — I could only apologize and wish the ground would swallow me. It was that blind spot where my ear for dialect should have been. I expect it all ties up with my not having an ear for music either. I do sing quite a lot actually, but even the cows get restless. I like to go to church with Joan's cousin Bessie, who has a lovely voice. I stand beside her opening and closing my mouth, pretending that the soprano notes are issuing from my throat. Like a little girl I once knew whose hair never grew longer than a crew cut, and who used to pull her friend's heavy plait over her own shoulder and stroke it wistfully. My heart bled for that child.

Anyway the dilemma went on and on with Mrs Lytton's daughter's husband desperately and rather touchingly offering me words and phrases which I accepted, chewed on a bit and regretfully handed back again, until at long last the appearance of Mrs Lytton's daughter released us from the impasse. Her husband had been asking me, she translated, if there were fish to be had in the beck? Salmon perhaps, or trout?

The verbal blockage blessedly unstoppered I began to babble. Fish? Oh, dear yes. Yes indeed. Well, no, not salmon since a fall of rock some time ago—during the war, actually—stopped them getting up, but trout. Not a lot, mind, but some. Eels, now, lots of them. (This was the only information I was really sure about because Mr Boon's sons had been hauling them out all week. Come to think there couldn't be so many of those left either.) From this I proceeded to various methods of cooking eels, information also gleaned during the past week. I rounded off the whole lecture with a discourse on fishing licences and piscatorial rights, along with a magnanimous invitation to Mrs Lytton's daughter's husband to fish, by all means, whenever he liked.

Her husband, said Mrs Lytton's daughter, wasn't keen on fishing. He was a pigeon fancier himself.

He ought to have been at Westwath when Fair Rosamund came to live with us.

I was milking one evening when the brilliant sunshine streaming in through the small, high, glassless window in the apex of the cowhouse wall was suddenly partly eclipsed. There in the opening, poised like a dancer in *Swan Lake*, sunlight filtering through her feathers like an aureole, was a beautiful snow white pigeon. She posed there in the spotlight for a few moments then, having contrived an entry worthy of a prima ballerina, swooped down and settled on the low brick wall which divides the cowhouse in two parts, watching the proceedings with bright-eyed interest. Naturally I gave her a handful of corn and from then on she was usually to be seen strutting at my feet or hovering overhead, uncomfortably like a disembodied spirit.

She was always on the dividing wall at milking time, marching up and down like a guardsman on sentry duty, hopping onto the rim of the spare milking pail and cocking a disapproving eye into its void or dipping a blissful beak into the full one, until one evening she overbalanced and fell in. Milk showered over everything as she did an energetic butterfly stroke through the froth; from that time I had to remember to cover over the bucket.

One peaceful Sunday afternoon I was tidying the hayloft to make room for a new crop and Gordon and the boys were bent on their own occupations, when I was hailed by a voice from the direction of the footbridge. I knelt down and peered through the hayloft door.

'I want some honey,' peremptorily demanded the large woman who stood there.

Almost simultaneously, mother leaned over the garden gate and said that a gentleman from Skipton was at the back door enquiring about honey and she had told him we hadn't any.

'I'm sorry, we haven't any,' I called out to the woman just as the man at the back door yelled the same information in a startling voice that gave Jess quite a turn.

'Haven't any!' echoed the woman incredulously. 'Where's our Bill?'

Bill, it seemed, was crossing the wath, had asked Gordon if we had any honey and was conveying the news of the deficiency in the same tones with which the whole family was blessed. 'THEY HAVEN'T ANY, TELL MAM.'

'I know they haven't,' roared Mam. 'And tell Grandpa not to come down.'

Grandpa, it appeared, was still at the top of the cart track and his contribution could be heard as a quavering piping as he passed on the sorry tidings to whoever waited in the car.

Rivetted, I watched the scene from my gallery vantage point: Mam standing on the bridge in the attitude of a Wagnerian heroine, the supporting cast artistically disposed about the set with voices raised in full-throated chorus. Bill by the wath was giving it all he'd got as he unnecessarily passed on Mam's message to Grandpa, Father (presumably) still by the back door in strong vocal competition with Jess, Mam's vigorous contralto booming half a bar behind and up in the flies Grandpa was coming in like an answering French horn.

On second thoughts, perhaps it was more like an old Schweppes advertisement with yodellers perched on every mountain peak.

'They haven't any honey — any honey — honey — honey.' The words bounced like ping-pong balls from side to side of the valley as the family retreated up the track.

As the reverberations died away and the dust slowly settled, Fair Rosamund circled once and fluttered down like the dove of peace. We shook ourselves out of a spellbound trance and normality returned to Westwath.

Not that it was normal by other people's standards. We still had Fair Rosamund with us. She stayed all that summer, appearing in all places at odd times like our fairy godmother, posing in the sunlit cowhouse window, floating from apple trees in the orchard, daintily tripping about the yard . . . and streaking for her life with a dozen jealous hens in pursuit. Always spotlessly clean and dazzling white she looked like a princess among a rabble of street urchins until the day she blotted her copy book.

She had been missing since the previous evening and I was well through the second milking of the day when she quietly appeared on the wall. No coquettish hovering in the window that day. No guardsman parading and flaunting of feathers. This time she positively slunk in and tried to make herself inconspicuous in the lee of the milk pail. And no wonder, for she was as black as the ace of spades.

Whose chimney she had fallen down we never discovered but Binnie took one look at her and changed her name to Othello on the spot. She might have been a boy anyway, for all we knew. Mrs Lytton's daughter's husband might have told us.

15   Nature Is Basic

Will came with his tractor and grass-cutter and mowed the back hayfields on that first evening of the Lytton's holiday, and three days later the drying grass was ready for turning. It lay in long neat rows like brush heads by the yard, the bottom of the grass stalks thicker and lighter in colour than the tapering tops.

As soon as milking and calf feeding were over I shouldered a wooden hayrake and mounted the stone steps which lead from the garden to the main hay field, and started turning. The action calls for some skill which is only acquired by practice. Well meaning friends, calling in while haytime is in progress, join in with joyful cries. Just give them a rake, they say, and tell them what to do and they'll give us a hand. Then, after an energetic half hour or so during which someone gets the rake handle between her legs and falls down and someone else loses a few teeth out of his they say, now that they have helped us can't we all spare an hour for a cup of tea? At length they depart leaving tightly rolled ropes of hay which have to be teased out again with a fork.

In these situations diplomacy is difficult. When people phone us and ask if we are haytiming because if so they'll come and help us, we can hardly say, thank you but not just now as we're haytiming, can we? They might cross us off their visiting lists for good.

I walked along each row pulling over the swaths thick end first so that they splattered down, dry side under, exposing the fresh green undersides to the sunshine. Our fields are small — this hay field being the largest at slightly under two acres and roughly triangular in shape — but they seem as large as the Canadian prairie when haymaking is done by hand and every square foot of them has to be covered.

Fresh in the morning it was glorious. As I worked I occasionally raised my eyes to the surrounding moor where the skylarks sang. It was the only sound apart from the rustle of drying grass falling at my feet and the cackle of a hen in the farmyard laying an egg in Arthur Lytton's waiting hands. I was not alone, for Jess and the cats were with me, nosing into exposed fieldmouse nests and crouching in an interested circle around a dead grass snake. Jess would snooze in the shade of the hedgerow until my perambulations had put too great a distance between us, then she would amble over to a nearer shadowed spot and fling herself down again, and the cats, faroff kittenhood stirring their memories, would suddenly awaken into exhilarated action and streak across the field, bounding effortlessly over the hayrows.

At dinnertime I fed the calves and chased some wandering sheep through the cattle grid gate. Climbing the hill was something I could well have done without and the return to the hay field was not the joyous experience it had been in the morning. Now, the sun was high and hot, I was permanently thirsty, my shoulders ached and blisters were appearing on my hands. Jess felt she could bear our separation better than the merciless glare of the sun and chose to stay in the garden, a green oasis compared with the all over bleached effect of the field. Swinging the hayrake less easily now, I stumbled up and down the rows in ever decreasing triangles, keeping my back to the unturned centre which I was trying not to think about, and milking time came as a blessed relief. Farmers' rest, Old Rust had called it and, by gum, he was right.

It was cooler afterwards. The sun was dipping behind the top of the forest where trees diffused it, and some nasty looking clouds were gathering disquietingly fast, but with legs of lead, muscles like sprung elastic and blisters as big as gooseberries bleeding through their bandages, I could work no faster.

The Lytton family returned from their outing and Mr and Mrs Lytton accompanied me along the rows and chatted.

It seemed that a fishmonger visited our village on Wednesdays—news to me. He was called Eric (Mrs Lytton, in the dialect of their county which tends to ignore the letter R, pronounced it Oik) who, they had reason to believe, was related to them. They had seen him on his rounds and wanted to introduce themselves but the problem was, what if it wasn't he? The relative, that is. They couldn't very well go up to a perfect stranger and say was he Oik, could they? I saw what they meant.

By then the triangle of unturned rows was about the size of our living room carpet and I leaned my weary body on the rake and viewed them despairingly. Mr Lytton, bless him, removed the rake from my locked hands. Mrs Lytton turned me in the direction of home, told me to make myself a cup of tea and go to bed while they finished the turning. Thankfully I staggered off, not caring if they made the stuff into hay or old rope, though not to tea and bed because the calves were due to be fed again. As I dragged leaden feet down the garden path, the clouds which had quickly spread to cover the sky released their cargo and rain came down like stair rods: in the garden, beating the philadelphus petals to the ground and liberating their fragrance; in the back field where the cows sheltered beneath the canopied chestnut and the ragged robin and wild valerian glowed shocking pink in the greenish light; on the beck where the clear water suddenly turned opaque and, of course, on the hay field which would have to be turned all over again.

Though not as it happened for a fortnight because the rain, having started, seemed unable to stop. The Lyttons went home and a young couple moved into the bungalow. It was fortunate that they were on their honeymoon as it kept their minds off the weather. In fact I swear they never noticed it because at the end of the week when we commiserated with them about their spoilt holiday they merely looked puzzled and booked again for next year.

Day after day the rain came down, mist blotted out the hills and hay lay sodden and unworkable in the fields. There was one good thing about the enforced lay-off, it gave my limbs chance to recover. For days the family suffered with my aching, tingling arms and deadened right thumb. I amused myself by digging finger nails into my numb thumb, which caused a pattern of white marks but no feeling whatever.

Muscle fatigue, Gordon called it, and I wholeheartedly believed him.

Haytiming might be suspended but we were not exactly bored. Bluebell, after dithering about for some days, decided to have mastitis. At morning milking I discovered that one of her front quarters was hard and painful. Squeezing produced an evil looking yellow substance and a kicking hind leg. The vet when summoned gave her an injection and handed me a tin containing tubes of penicillin with the instruction that Bluebell's udder was to be stripped of the fluid and a tube squeezed up each teat, the udder to be massaged as much as possible.

Hesitantly I touched the painful quarter. Unhesitantly Blue lashed out an iron-hard hoof and spreadeagled me in the dung channel. This from Bluebell, who in the normal course of events never so much as shifted a foot a fraction, could only be an involuntary lapse of which she was already ashamed, so I wiped off the muck with a wisp of straw, righted the stool and settled again to the stripping. This time I never saw the lunge that felled me but one moment I was crouching beside the warm black flank and the next I was on my back beneath Rhoda, learning for the first time that she was white underneath, and for the umpteenth time that I was yellow. Cravenly I retired from the game and phoned Gordon.

The moment Gordon arrived home he started work on Bluebell, milking her out, administering the penicillin and massaging the affected quarter as Mr Taylor had instructed. For hours he crouched there — Bluebell, relieved of the putrid liquid, apparently suffering only mild discomfort — patiently working with one hand and holding a cup of tea in the other until night fell and his fingers seized up.

Next day when Mr Taylor visited Bluebell and pulled at her teat a stream of sweet white milk spurted into his cupped hand. He turned an astonished face towards me. It was absolutely normal, he said. He had been certain that she would lose that quarter and only Gordon's perseverance had saved it.

This success partly compensated for the failure with Flower. Flower was the sweetest little lamb imaginable. She had been born in the plantation that clothes Castle Farm's side of the Scar and borders Will's fields to the east, and Will sent word to me that he had seen a couple of ewes with their lambs in the forest and that one of the lambs was lame. Immediately I went off in search of them.

Unlike the wild wood through which our water is piped, this is a typical conifer forest with tall straight trunks growing as close as bristles in a brush, and unbelievably dark mere yards in from the perimeter. Almost immediately I spotted the sheep and was not overcome with surprise to recognize them as Christine and Friend. One of the lambs, a gimmer, (ewe-lamb) was very lame with a great swelling on its foot; despite this handicap, it easily evaded capture because it could penetrate where I couldn't, through the brittle black lower branches of the trees. The other sheep bounded ahead, pausing occasionally to allow the little one to catch up with them, then blundering on again. I followed as closely as possible but they were soon out of sight and earshot and I found myself alone in the gloom, hemmed in by a palisade of tree trunks and without any sense of direction. Not far away the Arrowsmiths would be going about the evening chores; Charlie Rawdon on his way to the pub would be passing Westwath where the children were setting about their supper, but for all I could tell in the silence of the forest the world's activities could be suspended and time standing still. I couldn't even hear the beck.

It seemed ages before I got a clue to my position. I had walked on hoping to strike a firebreak that would lead me out of the maze but before I did so I felt the ground shelving downwards and I knew I was heading for the beck. Sure enough the trees thinned out and became scrubby, and in the evening light I emerged onto a grassy shore where a few yards away Christine and Co. nibbled zealously. I hadn't a hope of creeping up on them and they had melted into the murk of the forest before I had taken a dozen steps. Flatly refusing to have anything more to do with the forest that night I continued to follow the beck. The sheep-shorn lawn almost immediately gave way to the giant-tossed boulders of the ravine, a drunken sheep walk staggering unevenly over the top until it was a mere scar across the face of the cliff. I crawled that part on hands and knees, clutching at stunted rowans and oaks which themselves were anchored only by the toenails, and tried not to think about the beck purling between saw-toothed rocks so very far below.

Next morning accompanied by Jess and carrying a bundle of straw, wisps of which I dropped at intervals to lay a trail, (hoping like mad that I shouldn't meet the gamekeeper who in all likelihood thought I was crackers anyway) I probed the forest again. This time, thanks to Jess and the straw, the mission was successful and the lamb brought home.

From then on Gordon devoted himself to her, dosing her with antibiotics, bathing the afflicted foot, washing her rear, for she was scouring badly too, and feeding her with glucose-enriched milk. A plant of the common comfrey, *Symphytum officinale*, grew conveniently in the garden, and if its old country name, bone-knit, was truly descriptive of its powers we felt that the leaves of this in her diet could only do good.

Mr Rust, we knew, was a great believer in the powers of comfrey. He used to boil the leaves and drink the brew, and how he escaped poisoning himself and the innocent victims of his persuasion, we never knew, for what he insisted on calling comfrey was the wild alkanet, *Anchusa sempervirens,* which rampaged all over the garden—nettles and scrap iron permitting. The true comfrey he dismissed briefly as the Russian variety. Both Rusts had a way of naming plants wrongly and wildly. They did it with an air of authority that brooked no argument but Mrs Rust's rare bamboo was quickly shown the door when I recognized it as *Polygonum cuspidatum,* the giant knot-weed with the triffid tendencies.

Despite weeks of care and love poor Flower died. Gordon was deeply disappointed and I wept buckets and grieved long for this, the gentlest and most blameless of God's creatures. Even the certain knowledge that had she recovered she would have grown up to be an infuriating old curmudgeon like her mother failed to lessen the sorrow.

At least Bluebell was herself again as was obvious the day I took them up to graze on the roadside verge. This is very wide because a few years previous to our coming, by the instruction of the council the field wall on the inside curve of the road had been set back to allow motorists to have an uninterrupted view of other motorists wiping off their headlights on the wall at the opposite side. The alteration sliced the rind off our Scar and top fields, inconveniently placing outside a spring and its containing stone trough.

The cows loved to graze the roadside. Not because the grass was any better there but the trouble potential was. Immediately opposite was the Browns' house set back from the road at the end of a wide grassy approach. Round the corner and up, the road was blocked by the cattle grid. Round the corner and down, the road crossed the beck by the attractive stone bridge.

The Browns' afternoon tea was regularly taken to the accompaniment of champing jaws when the Three Musketeers lined up and peered over the hedge with embarrassing interest. This was all very well nine times out of ten, for Binnie and Steven were very good friends of theirs, but on the occasions when the Browns were entertaining, people became disconcerted to find themselves chewing in unison with three eavesdropping bovines and would refuse another biscuit. As Binnie said, it didn't do much for their prestige.

The cows seldom went uphill to the cattle grid. For one thing, the verge there grew more bracken than grass and apart from standing forlornly by the gate alongside the grid and shouting to passers-by (who didn't believe them anyway) that they were really moor cows who had been shut in, there was not much they could get up to.

Their favourite occupation by far, that is the one that gave the most satisfaction because it disaccommodated the greatest number of people, was the skilful art of bridge blocking. Well up the hill, all three with heads down virtuously intent on stripping the verge threadbare, they would move imperceptibly downhill nearer to the bridge until a concerted, udder-swinging rush carried them over the last few yards and jammed them, three abreast in the narrow road between the parapets. Having reached their goal they jostled for position, changing sides and peering intently at the water like small boys spotting tiddlers; vehicles squealing downhill, rounding the corner and suddenly coming across them reared like startled ponies and stalled their engines.

Today, to celebrate her recovery, Bluebell went traffic stopping on her own. They were well uphill for once, innocently employed in sparing the roadmen the trouble of mowing the grass while I leaned against the wall and admired the effect of wet buttercup petals on shiny, black, liquorice boots when

Blue saw the car mounting the hill. Waiting until it was almost level with her she swaggered casually out into the road and put down roots firmly athwart it. Luckily for her the driver was alert and stopped the car inches from her thick hide. Steadfastly Bluebell stared across the road, patently lost in admiration of the ivy netting the wall there and thinking that those raspberry leaves looked good enough to eat, too engrossed with higher things to notice the car's horn blaring into her right ear. The driver grinned wordlessly at me through the windscreen, gently easing the car forward until it nudged Bluebell's obstructing length. Apart from a single swish of the tail as though swatting a not very bothersome fly, she didn't move a muscle, continuing to stare rapturously at the wonders of nature and chewing absently the while.

Released from my trance I bounded down the bank and beat her bottom with my fist. The car continued to nudge, the horn to blare and at long last Bluebell condescended to acknowledge its existence. Sighing patiently she turned her head to stare consideringly into the blank headlight and swivelled back to look reproachfully at me. Slowly lifting her tail she deposited a mound of garden goodness in front of the car, turned an angle of ninety degrees and regally moved back to the grass verge.

The cows didn't often go up to the road during those two very wet weeks. Sometimes the beck was flowing too deeply over the wath for them to cross. A few inches above normal and the current was strong enough to sweep a body over. Still the rain came down. The farmyard in July was as plothery as in February. Roses balled and rotted off, the long stems of my precious irises flopped contorted to the ground, their flowers mud-spattered and transparent like wet tissue paper. New grass began to grow through the sodden hay and our thoughts shifted from chagrin at having to turn it again to despair of losing it altogether. I must confess that for my part mingling with these emotions was relief that I should be granted a longer respite for not only was I still feeling the effect of my last hay-making stint, but I was suffering from a battered rib cage as well.

It was entirely my own fault, I freely admit. I don't blame Rhoda at all, although if she had come in with the others when called instead of messing about behind the fence at the foot of the forest and then dashing in late muttering that Rosie would be pinching her nuts, it wouldn't have happened. For, of course, Rosie *had* eaten the nuts and Rhoda, swiftly lifting her head from a fruitless search over the bottom of her pillaged bucket in order to glare accusingly at her so-called friend, caught me an almighty thump on the chest with her head and the back of her forward curving horns as I was still fumbling with the chain.

I staggered over to the low wall which Rosamund graced so often, and leaned over it gasping with pain, feeling as if every rib I possessed was in fragments and wondering who was going to look after everything while I was in hospital. By and by I began to feel better and thought I might be around a bit longer to throw my weight about and now, a few days later I was almost as good as new — except when I breathed.

16   While the Sun Shines

Uncertainly the weather began to pick up. Nothing as extreme as sunshine, but for almost two days there was no rain and on Friday Mr Rust appeared and said he expected Gordon would be haytiming at the weekend. I looked at the soaked hay and the battleship grey sky and doubted it very much. No sooner had he departed than the clouds started to sob hopelessly again.

Gordon spent the showery weekend fencing, and paddling in the beck in leaky wellies as he fixed wire netting across beneath the roadbridge to give the sheep something to think about. I hovered about for most of Saturday waiting for the new bungalow people who were driving down from Perthshire — after tidying the bungalow and finding that the honeymoon pair had gone off with stars in their eyes and the bungalow key in exchange for a fountain pen and a pair of dirty socks. On Sunday I harvested out of the garden eight barrowloads of the Rusts' old rubbish and tipped it in the beck by the corner of the wath as a foundation for a concrete reinforcement.

Meticulous inspection of Monday morning assured me that it was not actually raining so I ventured to hang out a line of dejected washing and after dinner, pushing daring to the limit, started work in the fields. The stuff on the end of the fork looked more like badly made compost than hay and cleaved tightly to the second crop growing through it. The roadmen had told me that up the road towards the next village whole fields of it had turned black and was going to be burned as soon as it was dry enough. That, I reflected, was the best thing that could happen to ours only I hadn't a clue how to start a conflagration in a swamp and anyway, ours wasn't so much black as dusky.

I was in the middle of the calf field (we were taking a crop off it prior to turning the calves out) dubiously poking and pulling at the mess and thinking that wellingtons were unlikely gear for haytime when I saw old Rust approaching the gate, scattering gloom like the ghost of Christmas yet to come. Like that phantom he had one hand outstretched and flapped it at the compost in ostensible disbelief. He could hardly speak, he was so shaken. Why wasn't it made, he demanded querulously. It should have been turned yesterday. His tone implied that no-one should be deterred from making good hay by a bit of a monsoon. Not even us. Why wasn't Gordon at home, he said, and I was to tell him to stay off work tomorrow and get on with it.

Mouth open but speechless I stared after his slowly retreating back, succinct phrases I might have used forming themselves just too late to be effective. Recollections of our first winter floated before me. A memory of a cliff-like stack where the hay knife had sliced through, streaked and patched with greeny grey dust. Wasn't that mould? I had innocently asked. Only in pockets, he had said, smiling up at me to see how I was taking it. Only in pockets.

'*Your* hay was mouldy,' I yelled, too late for him to hear, of course, and spent the rest of the afternoon muttering to myself and demanding of Jess what right had he to come here at all never mind talk to me as if I were third cabin boy of the *Bounty* and he was Captain Bligh.

I was still muttering when Robert came home from school and helped finish turning the field. I muttered harder next day when the heavy drizzle returned, but as least I could go to the village school Open Day with a clear conscience.

At last the sun shone, fresh breezes blew and against all odds the hay dried out. The minute he got home from school Robert changed into jeans and joined me in the fields, beating Pauline only by the time it took her to run the half mile downhill to our spot. Gordon commenced his summer 'holidays' exchanging a spray-gun for a hayfork, and Binnie, Judith and Richard from next door, Michael and Duncan from the bungalow and the Rankins, Mum, Dad and the two eldest girls who were also staying with us swelled the labour force to gratifying proportions.

After its unpromising start that haytime turned out to be one of the jolliest we have had. The hay, which was surprisingly good all things considered, was turned, windrowed, raked 'two into one', cocked and led. We became proficient at loading the sledge to maximum capacity without losing the cargo. First a cock on each corner like knobs on a bedstead, then the sides built up and the middle filled in, the heap rising higher and higher as the laden forks arched and descended in turn, like typewriter ribs. Now and then some of us would try to carry too large a cock from too great a distance, staggering to the sledge on fast-buckling legs, and it would slip off the prongs and cascade over our heads smothering the smaller fry completely. Sharp bits would penetrate our shirts and unidentified creatures with legs creep in our ears, and it was all very pleasant indeed. Gordon on top of the stack was bombarded with hay from all sides and he pulled it in, spread it out and trampled it firm, always finding room for more. When it seemed that another straw would break the camel's back someone would call, was it a load? Usually, according to Gordon, it wasn't and he would find himself smothered by half a dozen cocks arriving simultaneously from different directions, but he never fell off. It was disappointing really.

He would slide down at last; ropes were thrown diagonally across the load and swigged on until the stack looked like an enormous hot cross bun. Pauline and Robert, sprawling under the sweeping hay skirts at the two rear corners, slotted the ropes through the end pieces and made them fast, convulsing legs and rear ends indicating the amount of exertion called for by the operation (how those kicking legs have lengthened over the years as they perform this annual ritual) and at length emerged, red faced and breathless, spitting spiders and sneezing hayseeds. The tractor took up the strain; a slight jerk and the laden sledge, looking like an overgrown Dougal, shambled off to cheers from the crowd. On arrival at the hayshed the ropes were released, and to make it easier to handle the top layer of hay was pushed off with a row of forks like tearing the crust off old-fashioned bread. Then while some tossed it inside, others hoisted it up to the top of the stack where

107

Gordon once more waited to receive it, all working like billy-o as we pushed the rustling, scented harvest into corners. Then we jumped on it, picking ourselves up from under over enthusiastically aimed loads, going down again beneath the next and rebounding as if on a trampoline, searching for lost shoes and belts and on one occasion a person, who had vanished down an air-shaft. Finally Gordon suggested that we might be a little over staffed for this part of the business and tactfully despatched a detachment for liquid refreshment.

As I say, it was a jolly haytime and all would have been as merry as a wedding bell if it hadn't been for the spectre at the feast in the shape of the ageing eccentric Fordson tractor. It had cost us only twenty pounds so we had not looked to it for over generous co-operation but we had not bargained for its requiring three days' notice in writing before it would start. Preparing the tractor for major jobs like muck-spreading or haytime was on a parallel with the activity which goes on at the Royal Mews before a coronation but seldom is a coronation procession halted by a radiator spraying water like a stirrup pump and never does a royal car wear an upturned bucket over its exhaust pipe to catch the sparks. Our tractor did. The bucket was clapped on whenever the tractor stopped, otherwise the unwary were peppered with shrapnel and embers. It was a lovely display at night. Because of its artistic talent for these firework displays with sound effects reminiscent of World War Two, the tractor threw deplorable temperaments. Wild exclamations, sobbing and shaking developed into mounting hysteria until it fainted dead away in the middle of the wath with the beck rising, or when crossing the road after nightfall with no lights and an unsteady last load of hay. We also reaped a crop from the two high fields over the road, and no-one was more relieved than I was to see those rococo scrolls go down before Will's blade.

By this time friends of ours from Hull were occupying the bungalow. Tom and Frankie spent almost their entire week's holiday in the high hay fields walking up and down, round and round, turning, raking and cocking. At breaktimes, sitting in the warm hay at the very top of the field we drank coffee or squash and ate biscuits and watched other people work.

Far across the valley and away to where the brown curve of the uncovered Roman road cut across the heather Mr Hewson of Rowan Head was turning, the lines of swaths changing from blond to brunette as the spinning tines lifted four rows at a time. Immediately opposite in the fields below Ellers House, Charlie and his stepson Tom were leading. A trailer stacked high with bales crawled up towards the farm buildings, two or three dogs describing daring circles around it while the gist of Tom's expletive reached us clearly across the intervening forest clad valley. Nearer at hand on our own hillside Joe Stewart had only just started cutting — that field was always late to ripen — but despite our head start, because of our slower hand work, his last load would be led simultaneously with ours.

Yes it was a happy haytime. Good companions leavening the labour as nothing else can do.

Tom and Frankie went home looking brown and healthy. They'd had a lovely holiday, said Tom enthusiastically. Walked miles and miles and seen some magnificent scenery. They had, too, and all in the space of the same two fields.

17   Angels Unawares?

Gordon spent the last three days of his holiday shearing sheep.
Will and George had offered to do this with their electric clippers but the road traffic was so heavy that week in mid-
August, that we dare not drive the flock up the road. Recalling the confusion inflicted on one inoffensive Mini by a handful, the thought of the chaos five dozen of them could churn
up amongst the holiday flow drained the blood from my head
and made me tremble all over. So we penned them all by the
gate in the Scar field where they stood calmly enough until I
went in to catch one. Then they pretended to think that I was
a wolf and rolled their eyes, milled about, climbed onto each
other's backs and brought down chunks of walling which fell
into what had suddenly become a quagmire, and I got all
mucky heaving them up again. Their curving horns, though
chiefly used for hooking into wellington boots, were heaven-
sent handgrips; I hauled ewe after ewe out of the mêlée and
deposited it at Gordon's feet. Spreadeagled ignominiously on
its back it yielded truculently to the big triangular-bladed
hand clippers which Gordon manipulated surprisingly expertly, unzipping its waistcoat with a steady hand and accurate
eye.

I could have a go if I liked, he said as I staggered back with
the next ewe. The ewe looked worried to death and well she
might, because unlike Gordon I am ham-fisted. I was also
frightened of hurting her and the resulting heap of wool pieces
looked like something even the rag and bone man wouldn't
bother to collect.

Charlie Rawdon, pausing on his way home from the village,
was so irritated he snatched the clippers out of my hand, said

110

give him 'od, he'd show me how to do it, and in no time had peeled back the fleece like the skin off a banana. The released ewe, embarrassment written all over her at appearing in public in her clean, white combinations disfigured by a new smear of red on the seat and a large red letter F on one side, trotted off with a toss of her head and great relief.

Charlie clipped another for good measure while I looked on admiringly and said that if he could do just one or two more I was sure I would get the hang of it. He wasn't fooled by this tactic, said 'Uh?' which is what he always said when he was pretending to be deaf, gave me a funny look and drove away in disgust.

So Gordon continued to clip while I caught, and we both perspired and stank of lanolin. Old Rust used to rinse his mouth with cold tea then spit it out because, he said, drinking made you sweat; as we knew we were going to sweat anyway, we felt we'd rather have something to sweat with and so consumed enormous quantities of orange squash.

At length the job was completed and the flock returned to the moor, the unshorn lambs fat and grubby alongside their mothers who, as Antony said, were now all horns and music.

On Monday Gordon went back to work for a rest and on the following weekend we gathered the sheep again, this time for dipping.

Our dip was constructed from an old bath sunk into the ground in a corner of the moor by the Browns' house. It was surrounded by another system of hurdles, rather like a series of lock-gates, which allowed the sheep to plunge singly into the cloudy evil-smelling water of the dip, scramble out at the other end, pause on a sloping concrete apron to drain and be marked on one horn with a splash of coloured paint, and the last hurdle opened to freedom again.

The coloured paint on the horn was for my benefit. A dab of blue told me that the sheep had been dipped so was not to be gathered in with the defaulters; red showed that they had had their jabs and green, that the boys had been castrated and turned into wethers.

I had long boggled at the various sheep terms and was utterly mystified when the same animal was in turn referred to as a tup-lamb, a wether and a shearling. Predictably, Mr

111

Rust's explanations shed little light, but just about this time I came upon a reference in *The Flockmaster's Companion* published in 1835 which clarifies the terminology no end:

The young male, while suckling, has the title tup-lamb and sometimes a pur-lamb, when taken from the ewe it is called a hog-tup, hog, hogget, lamb-hog or teg. When shorn a year and a half it is called a shearling, when shorn twice it is a two-shear ram. When shorn thrice a three-shear ram and so on. When castrated when sucking it is called a wether-lamb, afterwards until shorn, a wether-hog and then a shearling. In some places wether-lambs are called headers. The young female when sucking is called a gimmer or ewe-lamb, after it is weaned, a gimmer or ewe hog, a teg. In some places an old ewe is called a crone or drape.

So, you see, you've got to be all there with your coughdrops, particularly as up here a ram is called a tup, pronounced — wait for it — teeap.

Dipping time was a messy operation with a good chance of getting very wet so was particularly enjoyed by the children, our own and those of visitors, who joined in with gusto. They would take turns to push the animals' heads under with the business end of a broom while I prayed that they (both sheep and children) wouldn't swallow any dip, or if they did, wouldn't die of it. The whole family smelt of sheep dip for days.

Pity they had done away with the treadmill, said Gordon as he set off for work the next day. It would have been easier just to have climbed up on it.

A few weeks later we waved goodbye to the last of the bungalow people. It was good to have the place to ourselves again although we should miss the company of those who had been so agreeable, and the few that weren't had at least been diverting.

We had two seasons of holiday visitors behind us now, not only renting the bungalow but also, rather to our bewilderment, occupying a suite of rooms in the house. We hadn't intended letting the rooms. Our family was capable of filling the lot and more besides, but when we took possession of Westwath sixteen months before, we were staggered to learn that along with the cows, sheep and bees, we had inherited the lodgers as well. The Rusts, fearing that they would never sell the place, had backed themselves both ways and had already let off the rooms for a few weeks, as in previous years.

We could hardly do other than honour the bookings and to be honest were not averse to the little extra income, but never having been a landlady before I was fairly shaking with apprehension as I met the first couple at the gate and preceded them to their suite. This was the Rusts' name for it, not ours, and if it conjures up a vision of something between Ye Olde Englishe Hostelrie and the London Hilton, forget it.

The suite was the living room, painted like most of the interior in light manure. It had somewhat darker walls from the smoke which puffed and curled through the gap above the canopy — in fact a narrow strip of iron meant to balance on the oven part of the range at one side and on a great ugly nail at the other: a typical Westwath arrangement. It was the back hall masquerading as a kitchen with a terrible old calor gas cooker whose accumulated rust of years had been inefficiently concealed beneath cream paint and a plastic washing up bowl sitting starkly on a wide lino-covered shelf. It was the bedroom above, eighteen feet long, three-bedded and painted *dark* manure even to the open raftered worm raddled ceiling through which myriads of moths descended like dustmotes from their breeding ground in the attic. The bathroom — and this was the rub — was shared with us.

The Bunthornes knew what to expect because, surprisingly, they had stayed here before. They considered themselves something special and it was with difficulty that I restrained myself from pulling my forelock and bobbing whenever spoken to. Mr Bunthorne bleated and the pretty baby girl cried on three notes. For all that the simple country life and even simpler country accommodation was very much below their standard they seemed reluctant to leave it. They hardly ever went out but devoted their holiday to bathing the little girl (possibly because of the living room smoke) in the bathroom, which meant that none of us could get in to spend a penny. They departed after a strained fortnight in which we dismally failed to live up to them, leaving the china cabinet a sticky mess of wine drips which brought the varnish off, and our family in desperate need of baths.

They were succeeded by the Brambles, to whom we might have taken more kindly had they not also had this unnatural bathroom obsession. Many a happy hour they spent in its sunny ozone filled fastness. Mrs Bramble, who was a compulsive laundress, sang joyfully as she plunged her arms into the wash basin and ran off all the hot water, even on their first day achieving two pairs of underpants, two pairs of socks, one tea cloth, one heavy woollen jersey and two pairs of jeans which seeped off the clothes-horse and onto us in the kitchen below. Why she would not hang her washing on the line in the garden we never fathomed. I think she was so fond of it that she liked to have it near her — which was usually in the bathroom with her family.

There is a step down into the bathroom and the Brambles made it a point of honour to jump off it, vying with each other to leap the farthest. We could always tell where they landed by the spot on the kitchen ceiling where the plaster flaked off. We shovelled fuel into the boiler like Casey Jones on the Cannon-ball Express in an all-out attempt to keep up the water temperature, dodging the plaster and laundry drips that fell about our ears like summer rain, while the Light Brigade did their stuff above us. It sounded as if they were dismantling the hot water tank and trundling it downstairs.

'When am *I* going to get a bath?' howled Gordon, kneeling down and reaching a long arm into the airing cupboard to feel if the hot water tank was warm. (Mother, with shorter arms, had just been up there on the same errand and had come down to tell us in an awestruck voice that she couldn't find it. We told her not to be so silly, eyed each other speculatively and dashed upstairs to see.) When I told Gordon he would have to wait until the folks had gone, I thought he would have an apoplexy. He recovered a little when I explained that I meant when they had gone out and not at the end of summer, which was what he'd thought I meant. Though the way things were going it seemed to amount to the same thing.

The minute they did go out, around teatime, all of us except Roger (very sensibly wearing nappies) fought our way upstairs and got jammed in the doorway.

If it hadn't been for the bathroom we might have got on better with them and overlooked the inroads they made into our woodpile. August it might be but roaring fires they were going to have and we could tell the time by Mr Bramble striding from our fuel store with a brimming coal bucket clasped in his arms. What shook Gordon to the core was coming across Mr Bramble laying into the woodpile with the long-handled axe which he, Gordon, had hidden for safety on the outside lavatory roof. What Mr Bramble had been doing on the roof of the bungalow's loo boggled the imagination, for the axe could not be seen from the ground as I knew well, having been searching for it myself for days. I suppose after that we ought not to have been surprised when he found the whereabouts of the spare calf buckets and swiped one for his son's tiddlers, or sniffed out and helped himself from the cupboard where the toilet-rolls were stored. If only they would *ask*, we would cry.

If we hadn't been yearning for a good wash we might even have forgiven them for reducing the garage field to a rutted grassless waste. Binnie and I were hacking through nettles in the orchard, inspecting the ancient fruit trees and deciding which gaunt stumps should come down when we heard the engine revving and roaring and were convinced it was a road rally screaming past. We congratulated ourselves that it was happening in daylight and not as was usual in the small hours of a sleep-shattered night, so when we wandered across the footbridge — pointing out to each other the little brown trout hovering and darting in shadowed caverns — and saw who it was and what they were doing, I was almost fit to be tied. There was the Brambles' car with Mrs Bramble, until that afternoon a non-driver, at the wheel tearing round and round the rapidly deteriorating pasture, scattering large lumps of it at every sharp bend. It was a good thing it was their last day or I might have been driven to do something fiendish, like locking her in the bathroom with a heap of dirty washing and the water turned off at the main.

They left the next day without, as mother had confidently predicted, washing the sheets first, and we waited courageously to learn what further crunch fate had in store for us. We had reason to think it would be a good one because the next couple had five small children, and how the bathroom was going to cope with that lot we couldn't imagine. The bathroom having become a pathological fixation we took it in turns to spend all the short interval between tenants in it, confident that we should see it no more until the following Saturday. But in that we were quite wrong. The Cherrys were a charming family from Halifax. Mrs Cherry had been a kindergarten teacher and, by gum, she had those infants organized so that they ran on oiled wheels.

Up in the morning and into the bathroom. In, out, in, out, one, two, three, four, five. Downstairs, everyone, quietly now. Everybody sit. Who's for an egg? Who's for cornflakes? One, two, three, four, five. Everyone to the toilet before he goes out, one, two, three, four, five. It was absolutely fascinating and they were all trooping off for the day before you would have believed it possible.

We were genuinely sorry when they left at the end of a really happy week but were just as lucky with the next arrivals, Barbara Bruce and her five year old daughter, Judith. We didn't know it then but this was to be the first of many holidays with us, renting the bungalow when we gave up the 'suite' and one year, when the bungalow was already booked and friends were staying in the spare room previously occupied by the Bruces, camping in a handsome blue tent in the nettles by the vegetable garden. They never seemed to be in the bathroom at all but shone just as brightly as the Brambles.

Mrs Bruce was a nursing Sister. The daughter of a country clergyman, she had had the sort of upbringing where blasted gates were unheard of yet in spite of this was immediately at home here. It was she who had helped with Twiggy, she who had with unfeigned interest discussed the workings and explored the layout of our drains when Gordon apologetically and with some embarrassment had had them up to investigate a stoppage. It was she, also, who helped with the round-up one dark night when Binnie and Judith came down to tell me that a motorist had knocked on their door and reported that cows were on the road. Gordon was visiting a farmer at the far end of the village and couldn't be contacted – I still had to learn that Gordon was always unreachable when crises occurred – and my herdswoman experience was still very limited, so I was glad of the trio's support when on trembling legs I ran to the road visualizing in glorious technicolour the carnage and destruction which undoubtedly awaited me.

At first we couldn't see any cows at all, *in extremis* or otherwise, until the reflected light from the headlights of a car descending Westwath Bank cut out from the dark backcloth the familiar shape of Bluebell filling the roadbridge like a cork in a bottle and apparently asleep on her feet. As we ran towards her a shadowy form came lumbering up to the road from the path by the beck, and Rosie had joined the party. Heavy breathing and what sounded like saplings snapping like rhubarb indicated that if there was going to be chaos Rhoda wasn't going to shirk her part in it. And the headlights were now sweeping round the corner.

I met the car on the bend only yards from Bluebell's body. The driver turned white as a sheet when he was suddenly confronted by a madwoman flapping a cardigan at his windscreen and sat there looking stunned as we four rounded up the unrepentant herd and drove it back to the night nursery.

Mrs Bruce had been truly initiated into Westwath ways.

18   Nothing Ever Happens in the Country

By the end of that second summer we sadly accepted the fact that the sheep were too much for us. Had the holding been large enough to support a family of six without Gordon's additional occupation, it might have been different. As it was he did a full time, physically demanding job with an hour's driving at both ends of it and I, as well as tending sheep, cows, calves and poultry, with spells of fencing, ditching, hay-making and gardening as light relief, still had to wash and bake almost daily and do the hundred and one household chores connected with home and family without even the benefit of electrical aids. So it was that after much heart-searching and discussion with the neighbours (who told us straight that we would never make anything of the Westwath flock anyway) we decided to sell the sheep at the annual October sale.

As the day of the sheep sale drew nigh Jess and I started our last full-scale gathering of the flock and as if it knew that its time was running out, every last ewe and lamb pulled out all stops to complete my demoralization.

Twiggy and the other pet lambs had been promoted to the Scar field where they lived a life aloof from the field's other occupants, always grazing together in a group and presenting snooty woolly bottoms to the rest of the flock. Ever one for knowing my own mind, one day I hugged the lambs to my bosom, vowed my undying love and swore I could never part with them; the next I was scouring the moor for escapees and calling down curses on their heads for all I was worth.

Never had they caused so much trouble. They crammed a year's devilment into three days, using every wile and cunning wheeze to get out and away. They jumped over the wall in dozens and scattered to the ends of the earth. They got down the Scar and pretended to be rocks or crossed the beck and melted into the forest and one day just as I was setting off for the village they performed such a neat piece of trickery that I thought my brain had gone at last. One moment I was walking along the road watching the lambs pottering about the Scar field while their elders snoozed or nibbled in the top field next door, and a minute later I had reached the cattle grid, glanced casually over my shoulder and nearly had a fit.

The top field was empty. Clean as a wiped slate. As devoid of life as the surface of the moon. Of those fifty odd ewes, not a whisker remained. For an age I stared with eyes like organ stops at the unbroken sweep of grass and the deserted road beyond until I suddenly remembered the lambs. Wondering if they too had been spirited away or were at this very minute being sucked into an invisible vacuum cleaner, I tottered across and peered apprehensively over the Scar field wall.

The place was as crowded as Trafalgar Square on VE night. Sheep littered the ground like kapok burst out of a cushion. They looked as if they had been there for hours. Lying down, they were, with eyes half shut, jaws grinding away as usual. I went on to the village in a trance.

We had arranged with Will to transport the flock to the sale and on the last morning before that day, as I was cutting thorn bushes and ramming them into other thorn bushes which stuck out from more thorn bushes between the barbed wire and the field walls, he and George sauntered up cracking hazel nuts with their teeth. They had been along t'Scar, they said, and ower t'moor in case any of our sheep were still out, but had only spied some of Alfred's. They eyed my defences admiringly and on the other side the sheep patiently waited for us to depart so that they could escape again.

Will spat out a mouthful of shells. Tak yowes noo, if I liked, he offered. Drive 'em up to Castle Farm and put 'em in Little Garth for t'neet. They'd be all right theer, looks tha, and they'd load straight onto waggon in t'mornin'.

I all but fell on my knees and kissed his hand. George opened the gate; Lassie ran into the field and, by divine inspiration it seemed to me, scooped out the ewes from the lambs and spilled them out onto the road where Will and George, standing in a heap of nutshells awaited them. All I had to do was station myself by the bridge to block the escape route to the Scar while the river of sheep flowed past me and up the hill for the last time. From now on they were someone else's responsibility. Carelessly, I pulled down a spray of hazelnuts and bit on one, all but dislocating my jaw. I had toothache for the rest of the day.

The day of the sheep sale was terrible, a day borrowed from November, dark with mist and grey curtains of rain. The sheep-pens were a quagmire in which the lambs slipped and floundered, their fleeces black with wet and mud. It was a pig of a day and about the most miserable we had spent in our lives. I didn't go to the sale. I couldn't face it. My goodbyes had been said the day before when no-one could see me howling into Twiggy's wool, and I stayed at home and left the dirty work to Gordon, as usual. We didn't have even the compensation of a worthwhile cheque as the sheep had brought very little, and we went to bed to toss and turn in an endless sleepless night.

But despite the worry and heartache, despite the incredibly hard work and the monetary loss, we had no regrets. Our life with the sheep was something we wouldn't have missed for anything, a full, rich experience shared by comparatively few and awakening a deeper appreciation of the significance of the Good Shepherd. What a trying lot we, His flock, must be.

For the best part of a morning searching for stragglers, for a day and a night's grazing for fifty ewes, for three journeys transporting the flock to the sale ground, Will charged us nothing at all.

If neighbours couldn't help each other sometimes it was a bad thing, he said airily, and I felt like going into a corner and howling some more.

Autumn that year was a bonfire of vivid colours, the grey tracery of trees which had already lost their foliage like puffs of smoke among the flames. Chestnuts dropped their leaves in a single night, the larches briefly regained their brilliant spring green before turning gold and shedding needles like moulting doormats. The entire surface of the beck became a gaudy mosaic in green, yellow, bronze and red—leaves of all

120

shapes settling, drifting, dovetailing together, overlapping and packing, stacking in layers like pages in an enormous tome against the wath and stopping up the pipes. I forked them out in heavy, weeping wads and barrowed them to the compost heap, load after load after load.

Another year would soon be over but not before I had narrowly escaped being taken into white slavery, or something. To be honest, I may be mistaken about this as to this day I have never been sure whether his intentions were honourable or not, whether I was receiving a proposal of marriage or the other thing.

The whole lurid incident took place at a time when Gordon was away down south on a course connected with his job, and mother was having a spell in York staying with my cousin.

The fact that I was holding the fort alone was a stimulant to the imagination and while I accompanied Rhoda in a St Bernard's waltz in the cowhouse I dreamed about what would happen if we got snowed up and the telephone line came down and Bluebell calved (she wasn't due for another seven months but I wasn't going to let trivia spoil a good story) and I had to cope with milk fever, leaving the boys alone in the house, trusting that they would not upset the oil lamps and set the place on fire. Bluebell would have complications that hitherto only an experienced vet had been able to cure but, unaided, I would pull her through and when Gordon returned there she would be proudly suckling twin calves (even my imagination boggled a bit there). I, weary from a week of sleepless nights battling for Blue's life in the cowhouse, but as modest as ever, would wanly wave aside his praises and quietly disclaim the neighbourhood's admiration. Come to think, perhaps the boys *would* upset the lamps and I would bring the blaze under control between bottles of calcium.

Anyway, there I was cosily milking and dreaming when I heard the sound of a heavy lorry stopping by the top gate, a door slamming and a man's voice calling. Wallowing in my reverie I ignored it for a while believing it to be a couple of acquaintances meeting on the road, night-time visitors to Westwath being so rare as to be negligible, until the sheer persistence of the voice finally pierced the neighbours' tributes. I carefully placed the milking pail on the dividing wall, shoved open the lower half of the door and stepped outside. At the top of the steep cart track the vehicle's lights illuminated a filigree of bare branches.

'Hallo?' I called tentatively.

I can report the ensuing conversation verbatim as my diary reveals all.

'Hello,' shouted the man, relief at having at last flushed something sounding plainly in his voice. 'Is Mister there?'

'Sorry, no. Why?'

'Where is he?'

'Out,' I answered carefully.

'Oh, heck. Well, I've come for t' young bull.'

Now, we had just finished rearing a little bull calf for veal because it had been practically given to us. A beautiful Jersey, he was, like a little deer, and never will we do such a thing again because we felt like murderers of the basest sort when it went to the butcher at a few months old. We'd had difficulty in arranging for someone to collect it but it had eventually gone only a few days previously and I concluded that the voice now crying in the wilderness belonged to one of the people I had contacted in quest of transport.

'I'm sorry,' I shouted into the darkness, 'he's gone.'

'Who has?'

'The young bull.'

There was a pause here while the voice mulled this over before trying another tack.

'What's your name?' he shouted.

'Fussey'

'What did you say?'

'FUSSEY,' I bawled.

Another pause. I could imagine him trying to decipher his instructions on a grubby piece of paper, getting nowhere and deciding to have another go.

'WHO DID YOU SAY YOU WERE?'

I wasn't surprised that he couldn't believe he had heard aright. Few people do and we're resigned to it but I saw that we could be yelling at each other all night.

'Look,' I said, 'wait there and I'll come up.'

I unhooked the oil lamp from the smoked blackened beam and ventured out into the night. In the glow of the lantern my breath rose before me like a fog and I had to peer through it to pick my way through the farmyard mud. The beck looked uninvitingly black, silver highlights indicating where the waters parted to purl noisily into the pipes underlying the wath. Trees on either side of the cart track loomed out of the night, swinging by in the lamplight like ghost-train skeletons and vanishing silently into the darkness behind me. At the top, in the light from the headlamps, I could see the figure of a man leaning over the white iron gate.

The track is very steep and I reached the summit and breathed at him.

'How old are you?' he said conversationally through the steam. 'Forty?'

Now, as an opening remark between two adult strangers, said with serious intent, this seemed to me to be the most unconventional I had heard. It wasn't so much for its lack of polish that I resented it but because, dash it, he was right, I was forty. And if lamplight is as flattering as it's supposed to be he ought to have thought I wasn't a day over twenty-five.

I was now close enough to see the wording painted on the side of the lorry. 'P. Slatterly, Coal Merchant,' it said, and what I was doing discussing ages with a strange coalman who had come to collect a no longer existing bull at seven o'clock on a cold winter's night, I couldn't imagine.

Now he was telling me that he was forty-three. He was a widower. His wife had died a couple of years before and he was lonely.

I breathed my sympathy and wondered if he had called me out especially to tell me this; when he went on to say that he owned a five thousand pound house in Ugdale and had a good job, was his own boss, and had a son who needed a mother, I began to think he really had. Well, I was sorry that he was a widower and lonely but not as sorry as all that.

'My husband—' I began

'Have a Victory V,' he interrupted thrusting a handful of the little black gums at me.

I took them hesitantly, put them in my pocket and started again.

'Look here,' I said. 'I'm sorry that you've come all this way for the bull because it has gone. It went a few days ago. Somebody else collected it,' I persisted as I didn't seem to be getting through to him at all. He was telling me how he liked to stay at home nights and watch telly. He wasn't a drinking man. But pleasant though it was chatting of this and that in the freezing wind I still had the milking to finish and the boys to put to bed.

So I went on talking about bulls and he went on telling me about the garage he had built with his own hands until at last something of what I was saying began to make an impression on him. What was this bull I kept on about, he asked.

Something peculiar seemed to happen to my brain. It went completely blank except for a fleeting impression that P. Slatterly was turning into a caterpillar sitting on a mushroom and smoking a hookah. I stared at him bereft of words.

Then at last the penny dropped.

'Bull?' he said. 'I haven't come for no bull. Is that what you thought?' He suddenly flung back his head and roared with laughter, slapping his thighs and stamping his feet with delight. I edged back behind the gate, glad to see that Jess was at my heels. The man shook his head hard to recover his self-possession.

'I've come to collect your wool,' he said. 'The clip. I'm from Wool Growers—don't work for them really. Just helping out. Here, have another Victory V.'

Enlightenment dawned, swiftly followed by relief that there was a rational explanation for the man's visit. The fleeces, of course. They were tied up in a couple of wool sheets in the workshop.

Relief loosened my tongue and I quoted Gordon as I have never done before or since. 'My husband says . . . My husband thinks . . .' peppered the conversation all the time we were loading the fleeces on board. He was due home at any minute, I replied quickly when asked. Couldn't think what was keeping him and I must dash back to my milking.

The man looked at me sadly for a few moments. 'Just a minute,' he said and dived down behind the driving seat in the cab. 'Hold your hands out.' From a big square tin he poured into my palms a stream of Victory Vs.

As I finished milking and foddering up I sucked Victory Vs, after giving them some thought and deciding that they weren't likely to be drugged—as an enticement they were original rather than effective—and pondered on my whirlwind affair. It couldn't have been my breathtaking beauty that had attracted him because he could barely see me, my conversation had hardly been scintillating and I smelled of cows so I had to accept that I was a natural *femme fatale*—Some have it and some don't.

Come to think, I don't know what he looked like either. I might have missed something at that.

19   How Far to Ararat?

Laying the waterboard's main pipe under the beck was an interesting exercise involving lots of sandbags and a couple of assiduous water pumps that kept us enthralled for hours. It was also expensive on thirty-five mm. film because Gordon earnestly insisted that this was an occasion of local historical interest and should therefore be recorded. The interest so far has been very local indeed, most of Gordon's victims incomprehensibly studying what seem to be pictures of creatures from outer space wrestling with snakes during a monsoon.

At least they were right about the rain. November was crying its heart out. Fallen leaves were the texture of soggy cornflakes and there was almost as much mud in the kitchen as in the farmyard.

The attic resounded with raindrops pinging into Victorian bedroom crockery, ornate items in flowery patterns of blue and gold obligingly left behind by the Rusts and carefully placed by us under the gaps between the tiles. We emptied them each day at bedtime and once we had to leave our beds to do it again only a few hours later on a pitch dark night of storm and tempest. We collided with the wind on the attic stairs and it knocked us backwards, tossed us aside like toffee papers and tore through the rest of the house slamming every door in its progress.

Shiver his timbers, said Gordon as he battled his way off the top step, it was like rounding the Horn in a windjammer. It was, too. The attic was shipping it green, slopping in over the taffrail, missing the potties and seeping off into the scuppers. All hands to the pumps, cried Gordon in a voice that rose and fell realistically as he passed me a brimming wash basin. The atmosphere was clearly getting the better of him. Outside, storm-tossed trees creaked and groaned, we clung to the shrouds and feared for the mast and the roar of the sea pounded in our ears. That was indeed a sobering thought, for the sea should have been seven miles distant yet there were unmistakable sounds of crashing breakers that seemed a little over ambitious for our familiar beck. But the dear old beck it was as daylight disclosed, roistering through the orchard on an intoxicated rampage and high-handedly taking over the water meadows.

Round eyed I watched it as I went out to milk. Sagging jawed I stared as a spare length of waterboard pipe was swept from what in normal times was a position high up the bank when I returned.

Needn't bother to shave today, said Gordon complacently. We wouldn't be having any visitors in this lot. No sooner were the words out of his mouth than a hail from the footbridge announced the arrival of the postman. The lower five of the ten steps to the bridge were completely submerged so the postman performed quite an impressive circus act, climbing over the rail and balancing along the top of the orchard wall. He didn't mind Gordon's unshaven condition, having seen it before, but following on his tightrope came Derek the roadman; then our coalman and his son came to see how we were faring and to take in the sights until the disappearance of two more steps prompted them to make a hurried acrobatic departure.

Gordon and Robert went with them. Robert was going on the choirboys' outing to York that day. The bus wasn't due for another hour but by then, the way things were shaping, he would have to swim for it so Gordon hoisted him on his back and pick-a-backed him across to the road and dare-devil me clambered up onto the bridge just for the thrill of it.

It was a remarkable experience to see the water racing along only an arm's length beneath the narrow walk. Only the three uppermost courses of the twelve which comprised the wide central stone supporting pier were still uncovered, only two on the upstream side where the oncoming rush broke against it. I was gripping the vibrating handrail and slipping into a Walter Mitty fantasy in which I was Sir Francis Chichester sailing

127

Gipsy Moth across the Atlantic when Gordon returned.

'What cargo are you carrying, skipper?' he shouted to a passing tree trunk, and I could see that he would never be the same again either.

The alders and ashes which in normal times fringed the banks now marched like an avenue down the middle of a river that was three times its usual width as it was fed by dozens of upstart streams which zig-zagged down the hillside like white chalk scribbles. The sound of it was horrifying.

We scrambled back to what was left of the shore. Of the lowlands surrounding the house only the hay field was entirely above the waterline, and the hump of the glacial moraine in the Holme field swam like an island in an inland sea. The flood fanned across the farmyard sending exploring fingers along the uneven ground and we scuttled about dragging things to what we hoped was safety, for the most part rescuing things of little consequence and watching ladders and valuable timber pulled off the banks to swirl and vanish beneath the swell.

High on the opposite shore Will and George appeared, gesticulating and apparently shouting, but no human vocal chords could compete with that terrible uproar so we signalled dumbly in return. There was no access to the bridge at all now, not a step was visible and the lane which inclines from them up to the house was entirely filled with water. The calf field had slimmed to only half its width and the path, which led from it up through the wood to the lane by Ellers House, was a river in its own right. That shook me, I can tell you, because all the time that the dry land was dwindling I'd had that path at the back of my mind as an escape route without, I admit, relishing the thought of trying to drive the cattle up it.

This wood, separated from the forest by a chain link fence, is privately owned and intractable, the sort of wood which resents being owned by anyone and is inexorably determined to lead its own life. Even the path is only there by sufferance, hindered by low hanging branches, protruding rocks and quaggy pitfalls. During one Westwath holiday we had partly explored this wilderness while trying to follow the beck to a waterfall we had been told about. (We know now that there is no right of way along the beck and get mad with trespassers

128

trying to find one.) The trees were chiefly oak, birch and rowan hedged about with great thickets of hazel, brushwood and briar, all self-sown and many self-felled, their rotting, moss-softened boles and calloused contorted branches submerging in treacherous marsh in which, we later learned without surprise, cattle had been lost. It was a prehistoric landscape where undoubtedly monsters lurked and crocodile eyes watched from every turbid pool. We would have sworn that no other human foot had ever trod there or even knew of the place's existence. In the descending evening light we found it distinctly creepy. Hardly a bird twittered and nothing moved except the perpetually hurrying water but though the beck teemed over a thousand miniature cascades we saw no waterfall worthy of the name. Obviously we were not going to find it that night and it seemed to me that before long we should not be able to find ourselves, so we emptied our wellies and turned around.

Marching purposefully towards us, as if the marshy ground was a first-class tarmac road, arms swinging waist high, step unfaltering, was a tall Scotsman in a smartly swirling kilt. He gave us a pleasant 'Guid evening!' as he passed on his unswerving route. We smiled and nodded mutely, no less shocked than if we had met the Flying Dutchman, backed by full Wagnerian orchestration, sailing up the beck. We never saw him again either.

I could just see us playing hide and seek in the undergrowth with the calves and losing them for ever in the bogs and I fancied it even less when I saw the stream pouring down the path in a series of rapids. I only hoped, like Piglet, that somebody would do something soon.

I was just considering how long it would take to build an ark when Gordon called out that he could see a tidemark. I thought he had gone off his chump at last but patiently he pointed out that if there was a tidemark then the water must be receding to leave a tidemark, mustn't it? Only too thankful to forget about gopher wood, which is not plentiful at Westwath, I rushed to his side to see. Sure enough a ragged line of silt, twigs, branches and socks straggled an inch from the water's edge. I don't know where the socks came from. The river still rocketed along, brown, and foam flecked, as virile as

129

ever but the broad silver ribbons which had appeared so suddenly down the ribs of the hillside were already shrinking to silken threads. We were safe.

Miraculously all the buildings had remained dry. The hen house had had the closest shave but because it was raised a foot from the ground the water came up only to the underside of the floorboards.

Two big trees were down, a black poplar which had stood by the stream that flowed from the forest, and an elm which now straddled the beck alongside the still deeply submerged wath, their upthrust roots scoured clean.

While it had been at its height racing unconstrainedly through the valley, the river's tones had muted to a monotonous roar as though it was so confident of its own stupendous power it could afford to dispense with threatening language and was all the more awe-inspiring because of it. Now that some of its strength was sapping it began blustering again, threshing and tumbling like a child with the tantrums. But it had lost its power to intimidate for the margin between the flotsam and the water widened hourly. In places the river was already back between its banks and the footbridge steps were reappearing one by one. By the time Robert returned from his outing, early in the evening, the beck was much the same as he left it and by the following morning it was down to its customary respectable proportions. But, by gum, you could see where it had been.

The fallen elm had collected enough twigs, branches and rubbish to make homes for a colony of beavers. It also embraced a drowned sheep. The five-barred gate by the bridge had gone and so had Gordon's ladders and various things that were not missed until they were needed.

Eventually the gate and a ladder were recovered still intact by the roadmen, found abandoned high up the rocky face of the Scar. The roof ladders Gordon found more than a mile away at the other side of the village.

But the rain had gone at last and on a crisp, sunny, windy Sunday Gordon and I passed through the gateway by the Browns' house and walked up the track to the moor. On the skyline the jumbled grey rocks of Killin Crag rose like battlements above the tattered red bracken which swept down to the narrow road that leads to the head of the valley, resumed on the near side and washed into the dark billows of heather rolling up to meet it. The russet and charcoal, streaked here and there with bleached bent grass, stretched to the horizon to fuse with its counterpart on the opposite hillside and between, like a bright patchwork quilt slipping down off sombre-hued army blankets, lay our tiny fields and those of our neighbours.

Not a sheep moved in all the empty landscape. It was tupping time again and the ewes had been gathered in, their absence dismally emphasizing the disappearance of our own flock. Only the inward eye could see the undulating rivulets running before the dog, the defying stamp of a forefoot when Jess got too close, the challenging lift of the head by a possessive mother of a new lamb. We should be glad when tupping was over and the moor populated again.

Up here the wind thundered on our eardrums despite anorak hoods and flattened us to the wall when we paused to look over it. Below, the beck, unashamed of past behaviour, glinted vivaciously as it wound past our farm buildings, and the house, snug in the rumpled quilt, looked contented and protected from the elements. It was a different world down there.

We gazed at it proudly, secure in the knowledge that it was entirely ours and well worth working for. Many toil filled days were behind us but now that the sheep were gone and there was only the cattle to care for we confidently faced a future of more leisure, peace and serenity.

Suckers.